MW00609361

AND PARTNERS

TASTE CRAFT & WIT

ASSOULINE

INTRODUCTION BY DAVID SCHIMMEL

TASTE CRAFT & WIT

ASSOULINE

FOREWORD

Given that graphic design emerged very early in the development of prehistoric cultures (as evidenced by rock and cave paintings across many parts of the world), delivering 20 years of brilliant design may not seem like a major achievement; yet when considered in the context of our highly disrupted and ephemeral modern society, two decades of business success is a remarkable feat of endurance. In fact, 20 years is nearly three times longer than most marriages in the United States and a few years longer than the average life span of S&P 500 companies. Arriving at this incredible milestone, in an era when closure is commonplace and even blue-chip firms disappear overnight, is a testament to the core foundational elements of And Partners: maintaining integrity in relationships while not only ensuring but enhancing the strength of all business propositions.

As one of the founding partners of the firm, I can personally attest to the success of And Partners being driven by the passion, humor and drive of its Founder, President and ECD, David Schimmel.

I vividly remember the moment I met David 21 years ago. We were both budding advertising execs at Young & Rubicam's Madison Avenue flagship. I was working in the Corporate Communications group, tasked with developing collateral for the agency's pending IPO. None of the creative teams I was part of had cracked the brief, so the CEO suggested I connect with this "brilliant new designer" she'd met through a special project on the most influential women in business. Upon meeting David, my own fledgling project took a positive turn: every no quickly became a yes, any drama turned into comedy and the belief that anything was possible became the standard approach. It's perhaps then no surprise that when David asked me a few months later if I wanted to break away from the big agency to start our own design shop, I jumped at the opportunity.

After a short time working as a young entrepreneur alongside David, I ventured back into the corporate world. Today I lead one of the top global advertising agencies, and am frequently asked to comment on creativity. To me, at its heart, creativity is the act of joining two or more often disparate things that were never together before. Creativity demands curiosity, bravery and a healthy disregard for the status quo. Few companies recognize its power and deliver it time and again as effortlessly and successfully as And Partners does.

Taste, craft and wit. It's so obvious: It represents the spirit of the firm's Founder. It represents the ethos of the entire company. And importantly, it represents the characteristics of work that will withstand the test of time.

Congratulations! On behalf of all creative professionals who appreciate taste, craft and wit, we look forward to the coming decades of work from the And Partners studio.

MICHAEL HOUSTON
Worldwide Chief Executive Officer, Grey Group

And Partners' original studio, 1999–2003, at 20th Street and Fifth Avenue

"THIS": And Partners' first portfolio book, c. 2001

&

Endless h
entertainm
21 authentic
ampersands.
NOTE: pencil a
not included. Id
Approved for age

45
&

46
&

47
&

48
&

39
&

56
&

57
&

49
&

58
&

59
&

67
&

68
&

And Partners' opening, 1999, self-promotion / party favor

urs of by yourself
nt. Includes all
And Partners
ace them all.
d eraser
l for travel!
10–110.

AND PARTNERS COMMUNICATION THROUGH DESIGN

Conference room detail,
And Partners' original studio, 1999–2003

blood
suffer
quiver
demolition
fury
excruciating
anguish
torture
infectious
prey

suffer

And Partners
156 Fifth Avenue Suite 1008
New York New York 10010
212 / 414 4700 ph 212 / 414 2915 fx
maureen@andpartnersny.com
Maureen McLaughlin, Associate Studio Manager

55

&

66

64

63

Oblique

And Partners 65 Bold
And Partners 75 Black
And Partners 75 Black Extended
And Partners 85 Extra Black

AND PARTNERS

156 FIFTH AVENUE SUITE 1234 NEW YORK NY 10010 WWW.ANDPARTNERSNY.COM
TELEPHONE (212) 414–4700 FACSIMILE (212) 414–2915

AND PARTNERS

156 FIFTH AVENUE SUITE 1234 NEW YORK NY 10010
WWW. (OR) DAVID@ ANDPARTNERSNY.COM
TELEPHONE (212) 414–4700 FACSIMILE (212) 414–2915

David Schimmel, President and Creative Director

AND PARTNERS

156 FIFTH AVENUE SUITE 1234 NEW YORK NY 10010
WWW.ANDPARTNERSNY.COM

Evolution of the firm's identity through the years
Top Left: 1999 *Bottom Left:* 2009/10 *Right:* 2004

is the mag...

FIGURE 5

But maybe being *new* annual report busine... such a bad thing?

AND & PARTNERS

156 FIFTH AVENUE SUITE 1234 NEW YORK NY 10010

We have enthusiasm, a fresh perspective and people who have done tons of annual reports in the past.

Just not here.

And to top it off, you can be assured you'll get plenty of our attention, because you'll probably end up being our second annual report client.

"5 is the magic number" annual report promotion, c. 2004, celebrating all things 5; illustrations by Seymour Chwast

Left: David Schimmel, President and Founder, in And Partners' second studio library, c. 2005;
Right: The firm's third office, c. 2009

And Partners' studio today in New York's Gramercy/Flatiron District

66 Art is what we call...the thing an artist does.

It's not the medium or the oil or the price or whether it hangs on a wall or you eat it. What matters, what makes it art, is that the person who made it overcame the resistance, ignored the voice of doubt and made something worth making. Something risky. Something human.

Art is not in the...eye of the beholder. It's in the soul of the artist. **99**

SETH GODIN

Twenty years later, I still can't believe that a chance meeting with Barbara Corcoran in the lobby of The Breakers resort in Palm Beach led to the creation of And Partners. Barbara sought me out during a "Top Women in Business" conference (I had created the identity for the event while working for Young & Rubicam) and asked me to rebrand her company, The Corcoran Group.

When I handed her a slip of paper with my number on it, she stuffed it into her bra and said she'd call me on Monday.

Two weeks later, And Partners was in business.

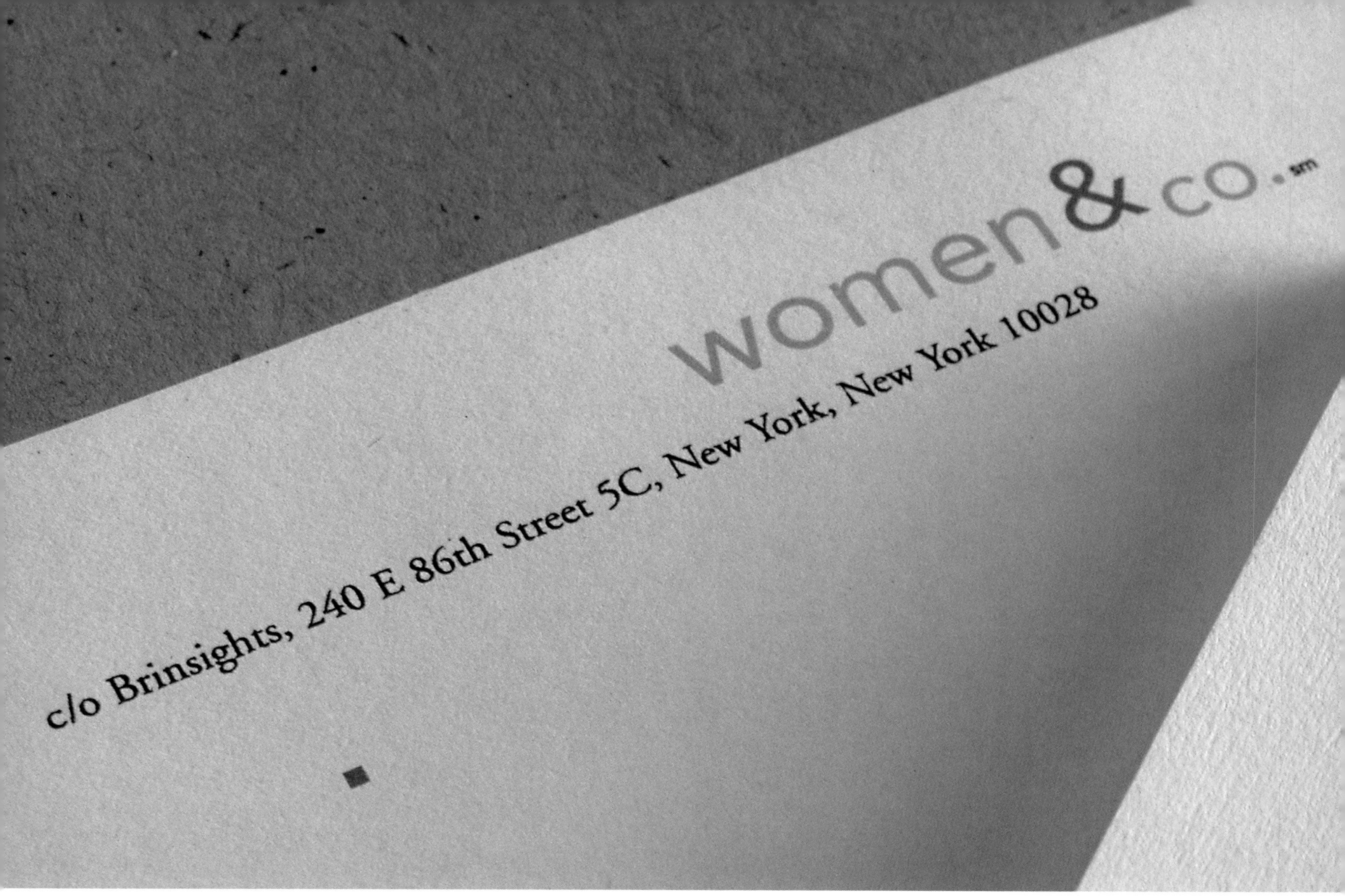

women & co. sm

c/o Brinsights, 240 E 86th Street 5C, New York, New York 10028

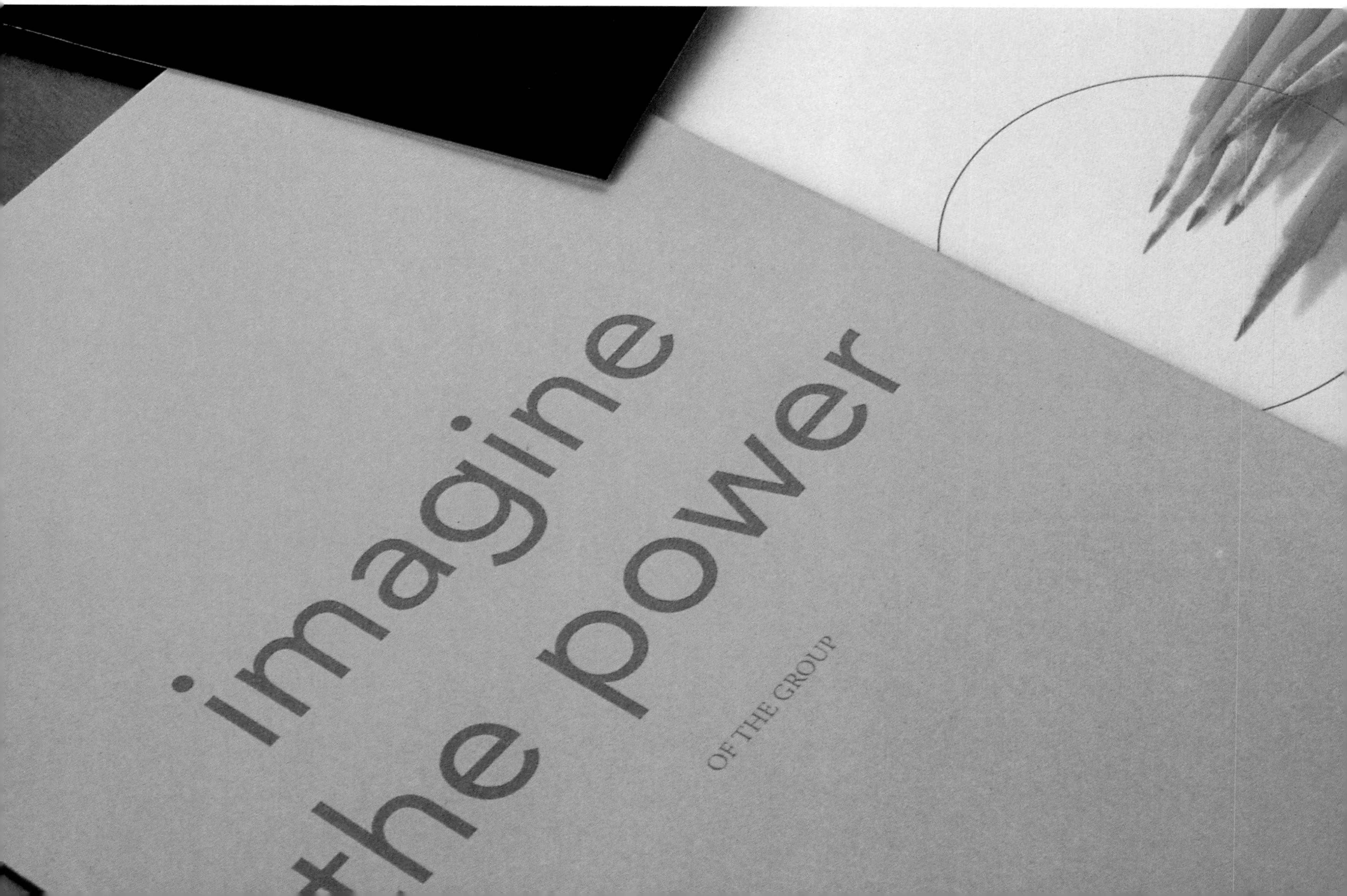

imagine
the power

OF THE GROUP

The Corcoran Group is revered as one of New York City's top residential real estate firms, known in the industry for its unconventional approach to marketing. And Partners branded Corcoran in 1999, from logotype and signage to advertising and promotion. The brand personality and tone reflects the image of the firm's founder and her role in relationship to the broker sales force.

the wordmark

Moving forward, we will refer to the company as The Corcoran Group in all communications. We will phase out the use of Corcoran's New York, as it is too limiting. By using The Corcoran Group consistently, we will emphasize the breadth and depth of The Group and the inherent value that the extensive network brings to our clients.

The entire wordmark expresses understated sophistication by using warm and inviting lower-case typography. The mark is a juxtaposition between plain and italic type and is an accurate reflection of the company itself. It is a little bit of everybody.

COLOR PALETTE

MARIGOLD
MERLOT
SADDLE
GLACIER

TRADE GOTHIC

TRADE IS A HUMANIST SANS-SERIF TYPEFACE THAT ALLOWS FOR THE SUCCESSFUL BLEND OF CLASSICISM WITH MODERNISM.

BASKERVILLE ITALIC

AN ITALIC TYPEFACE COMMUNICATES EXUBERANCE, LIVELINESS, AND MOVEMENT. JUXTAPOSED TO BASKERVILLE, IT EMPHASIZES THE CORCORAN NAME.

BASKERVILLE

BASKERVILLE IS THE EPITOME OF NEOCLASSICAL TYPE DESIGN AND WAS ESPECIALLY POPULAR IN 18TH CENTURY FRANCE.

the *corcoran* group
REAL ESTATE

The new corporate identity for The Corcoran Group communicates professionalism, expertise and market savvy as well as the company's creativity, playfulness and approachability.

It is not black and white.

It is about finding individual identity from within a group while maintaining a consistent, corporate voice. Rather than creating multiple systems of materials to appeal to specific demographics, this is a single system that is fresh, creative and bold. The solution– stylish, not trendy– will appeal to all New York prospects.

A modular approach to the identity's application allows elements to be mixed based on a desired communication objective as well as personal preference.

The varying needs of the group drive this identity.

In retrospect, my aspirations
as a 23-year-old were rather
grand and ambitious:

To create a new force in design,
in NYC, with the dream of making
meaningful and impactful work
that would capture the imagination
of my peers, colleagues and
the public. Work that would
intelligently engage its audience
and solve business problems,
while answering unmet needs and
desires. Work that would resonate
and withstand the test of time.

Designer-writer-
comedian-actor-
musician-quasi-vet-
erinarian-cow-lover-
mouth-breather-
gold-digger-shoe-
gazer-tree-hugger-
low-hanger-child-
bearing-lard-smear-
ing-drama-queen.
And you?

FIGURE &.—BIG FLAT LOOP SPOKE

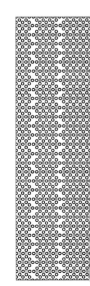

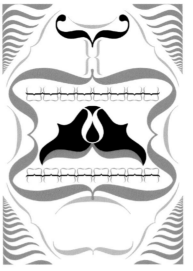

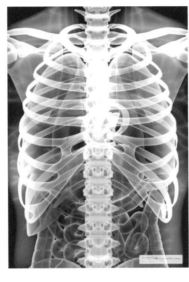

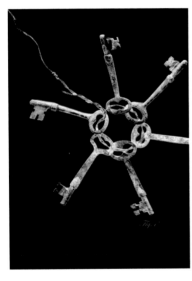

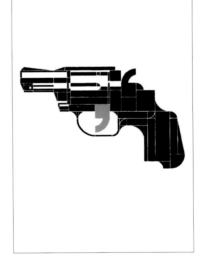
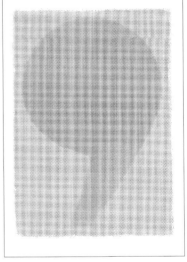
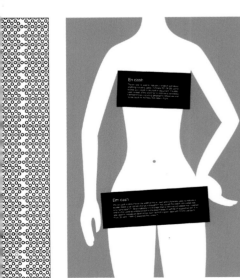

POSTER TITLE: *Figure &. — Big Flat Loop Spoke*

ORIGINAL MEDIA: *Oil pencil and photocopier.*

FROM DISHES TO DESIGN: *In 1994, I was a busboy at Planet Hollywood. In 1998, I was design director at Y&R Advertising in New York.*

MY LOVE FOR THE AMPERSAND: *It is not hyperbole, or even mild exaggeration, to say that I love the ampersand. I named my firm And Partners. The ampersand connects ideas or thoughts together. And, it indicates things that are additional.*

A NAKED AMBITION: *I founded And Partners with no partners and no clients.*

THOUGHTS REGARDING THE AMPERSAND: *Graphically, the ampersand got its start as "EL," which is French for "and." Depending on the typeface, this may be discernible. My copyright-free cowboy has a great grasp of his oil-pencil ampersand.*

AND ANOTHER THING: *The ampersand-as-lasso is wonderfully free-form, a sort of punctuation trial-balloon. As soon as it ropes something in, it becomes less visible. I could go on and on and on.*

FAVORITE PROJECT: *The SpecLogix Paper and Printing Compendium, a pair of comprehensive reference guides for designers, published in 2002.*

GREATEST ACHIEVEMENT: *Housebreaking Gordon, my Wheaton terrier.*

STRADDLING GOOD AND EVIL: *I try to balance work for corporate clients with projects for nonprofits and educational institutions.*

POSTER TITLE: *Untitled*

THE THINKING BEHIND THIS POSTER: *Unlike the period or a comma, the umlaut does not stand on its own — it requires a vowel to bring the sound to life. This poster was created while trying to create a visual feeling of the melodic sound of the umlaut — and the rippling effect that occurs when switching from an umlauted vowel to a long vowel and back again.*

BUSINESS CARD TITLE: *Art director, Martha Stewart Everyday Merchandising.*

AIMEE IN A PARAGRAPH: *My name is Aimee, and I wear a flower made of felt in my hair. I have never had a cavity, even though I love to eat candy. I can fall asleep standing up, like a horse. I have a fear of vomit. My favorite foods include freshly shelled green peas and chocolate cake. I wear socks that have toes, like mittens. I do not care for air-conditioning. I have a goldfish named Leon. I am a very fast reader. I like clothing that has zig zag stitching. My beverages of choice are sparkling water and champagne. I am inspired by life.*

FAVORITE PROJECT: *Over the past ten years, I have created a series of self-exploratory documentary projects that have helped to shape the way I view the world. With each project I undertake, I feel like I am*

POSTER TITLE: *"Tw...*

INSPIRATION FOR... *quotation marks to... state the poster's t... itself is. So it's both...*

ORIGINAL MEDIA: ... *composed in Adob... Powerbook G4...*

OPEN FOR BUSIN... *a design studio... everything; desi... odd jobs, etc.*

FIRST JOB: *P... design job was... Massachusetts...*

POSTER TI...

THE POIN... *metaphor...*

THE PO... *To creat... Catalogin... (BlackRoc...*

A FEW... *creat... Steward... Real E... Tinte... Design...*

COM... *fore...*

PO...

Figure &. — Big Flat Loop Spoke   DAVID SCHIMMEL

Semi Colon

MICHAEL...

---

rules governing the use of the comma, and not a one makes any sense. It's time we stopped taking the power of punctuation lying down. We should burn the apostrophe in effigy. And trash the dash. We should take a stick to the caret, interrogate the question mark, and stop listening to what quotation marks have to say. Punctuation needs to be dragged out of its ivory tower and made to suffer like the rest of us. Punctuation is either part of the problem or part of the solution, and brothers and sisters, from where I sit, it looks like the problem. So unite! Unshackle yourselves from the tyranny of the tilde. Tell the hyphen to take a hike! Let's string up the colon by its little balls! It's time to kick some asterisk!

Punc't

...ought
...y are
celebrated, ...
graphic designers in ...
asked to create posters about p... ictuation?
A stunningly beautiful limited edition
series of serigraphs: interpretations of two
dozen marks with which several of the
designers were clearly unfamiliar. (To be
fair, who among us can claim intimacy
with the caret? [Check spelling before
replying, please!]) The resulting images —
which will surely both delight and defy
grammarians — have far more to do with
creativity than literacy. Finally, our
cunning exhibition is capped by a delicious
irony — our proceeds will go to the charity
Books for Kids, whose lofty purpose is
to promote the most punctuation-driven
activity ever — reading.

Punc't was conceived by And Partners on behalf of Neenah Paper to help them grow market share in the highly competitive Northeast U.S.

And Partners art-directed a limited-edition series of 24 signed and numbered serigraphs on the subject of punctuation, and managed the overall project that culminated with a gala opening.

In addition to bolstering Neenah's sales efforts, the project has had a larger impact: Neenah and And Partners selected the Books for Kids Foundation to receive all of the proceeds from the sale of the work. Those proceeds have since built several libraries in the tristate area. Punc't also garnered significant press and industry awards (including a coveted One Show Gold Pencil from the One Club) and has been exhibited internationally. The works have been showcased in museums worldwide, including at MoMA in New York.

The Writing's on the Wall

Punc't

It's time we put punctuation where it belongs. Punctuation is language's dirty little secret. It's the tail that wags the dog. It's the vast conspiracy of silly little marks that's held meaning hostage for centuries. Well it's time we rise up and fight the oppression punctuation has lorded over our inalienable right to self-expression. We should burn the apostrophe in effigy. And trash the dash. We should take a stick to the caret, interrogate the question mark, and stop listening to what quotation marks have to say. Punctuation needs to be dragged from its ivory tower and made to suffer like the rest of us. Punctuation is either part of the problem or part of the solution, and brothers and sisters, from where I sit, it looks like the problem. So unite! Unshackle yourselves from the tyranny of the tilde. Tell the hyphen to take a hike. Let's string up the colon by its little balls! It's time to kick some asterisk!

DAVID
SCHIMMEL

And Partners survived the dot-com boom and bust of the late '90s, the false alarm of Y2K (no planes fell from the sky!) and the horrors of 9/11. We outlasted the Great Recession, while witnessing the rise and fall and spectacular resurrection of the real estate market.

We've withstood the many paradigm shifts that have changed the ways that business and life unfold—the arrival of Google, the reach of Amazon, the ubiquity of smartphones and the limitless capacity of the cloud. We've weathered the disruption of prime time and appointment viewing by DVRs, YouTube, Netflix and Hulu. We've adapted to how Facebook, Instagram, Snapchat and WhatsApp have altered the ways that people connect with one another, through personalized worlds. We've watched Dyson kill the vacuum bag, Tesla electrify automobiles and Peloton evolve fitness.

As people have come to expect everything to be available as a service, we've consistently created new ways to deliver.

Again and again, And Partners has proactively reinvented itself—sometimes out of necessity, oftentimes to remain ahead of the industry. Fortunately, design has progressed from being a nicety to fulfilling an essential need. Consumers have become increasingly design-literate and companies have become aware of the strategic and competitive advantages that good design affords their brands. The ongoing challenge for And Partners lies in navigating a fragmented media landscape and developing innovative form factors that are capable of commanding the attention and respect of skeptical consumers.

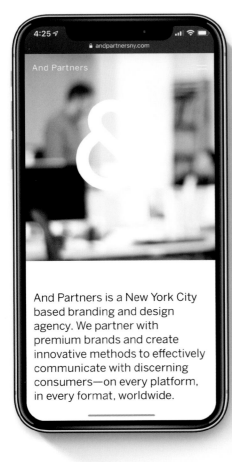

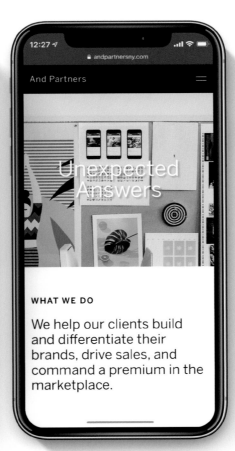

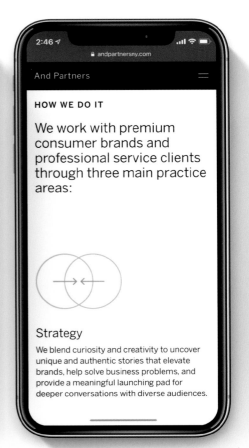

HEARST *app lab*

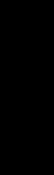

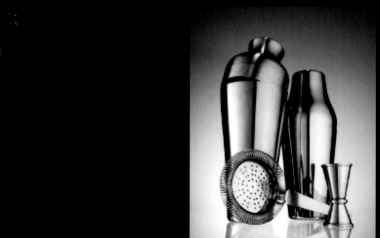

Hearst App Lab, a space for discussion and
innovation around smart mobile expressions
of branded content.

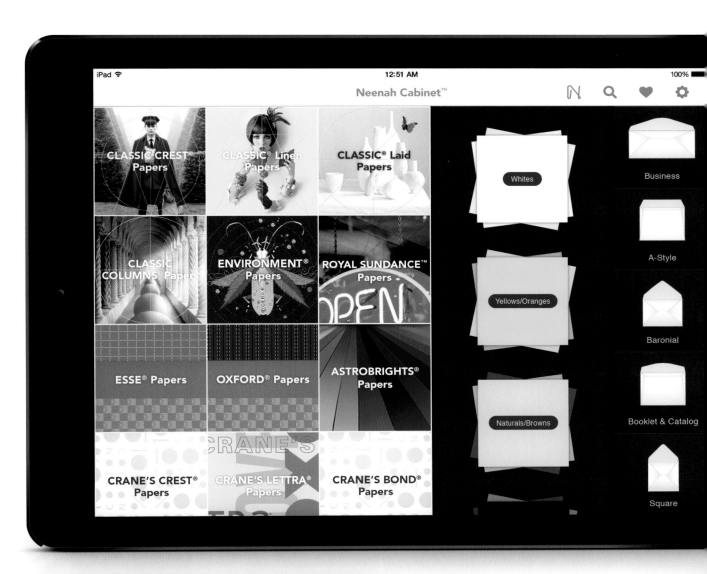

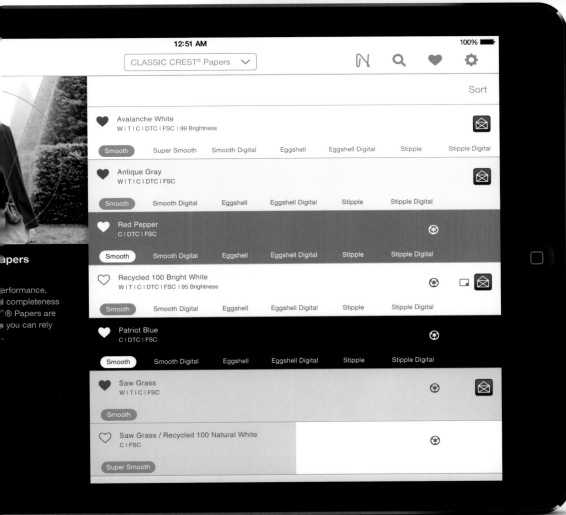

And Partners helped Neenah evolve from a traditional paper company into a communications powerhouse by combining strategic planning and innovative technology to reinvent not just their marketing communications, but how they actually go to market.

In 2012 Neenah Paper introduced Cabinet, the first iPad Application for Paper Selection, followed by a complete cross-platform solution, under the same name, for Mac, iPhone and Android devices.

As our work becomes increasingly sophisticated, all-encompassing and strategic, it can only be made by teams that meet the highest production values to match the desired deliverables.

We have transitioned from selling artifacts to formulating ideas. Our work has also advanced from singular, iconic designs to systems that are dynamic and changing, usually optimized for digital, with mobile being the most critical medium—for now.

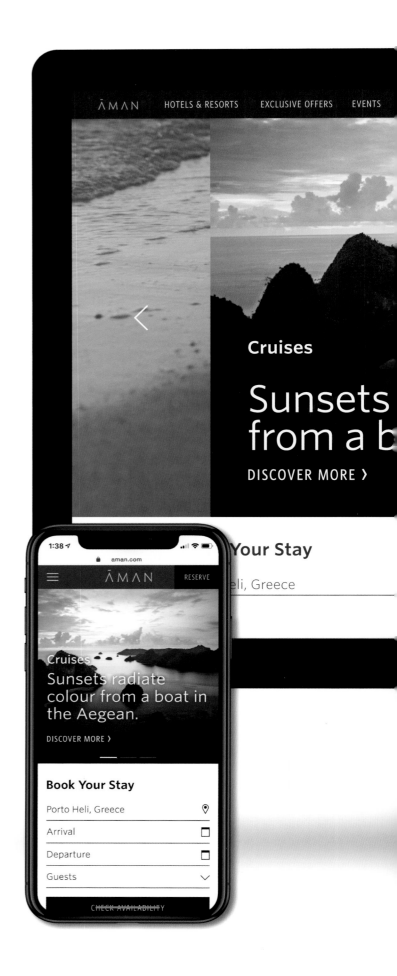

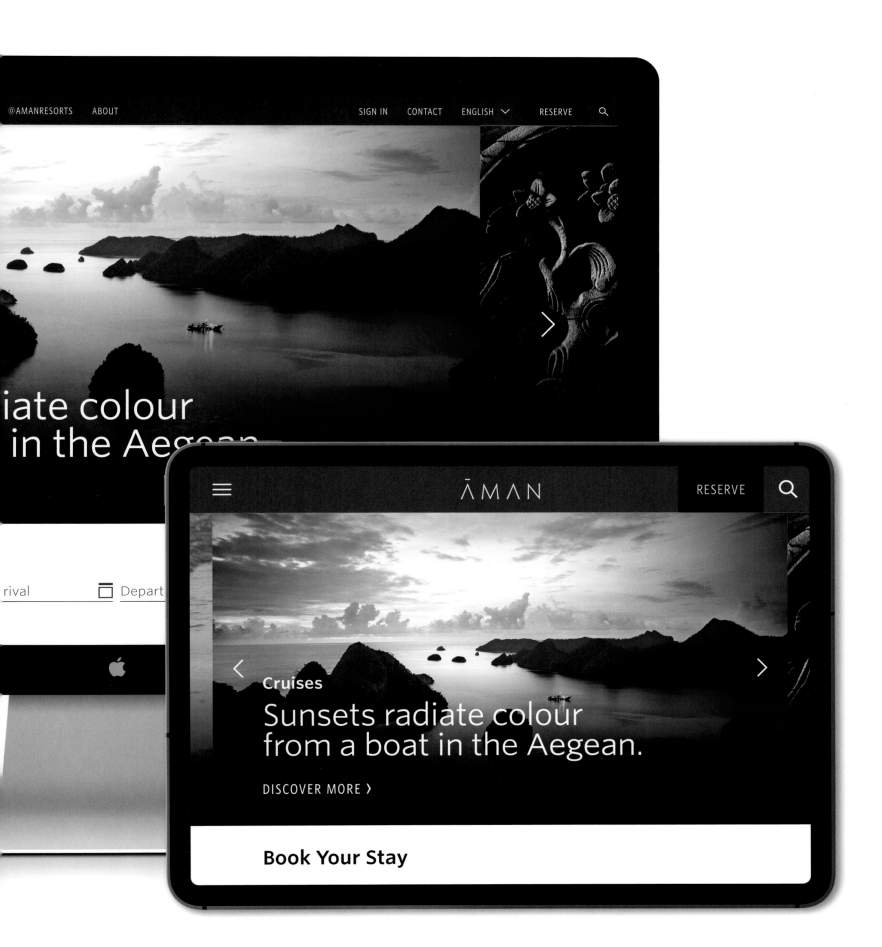

Āman.com, public website design 2017.

Āman, one of the world's premier hospitality brands, has a loyal set of followers and takes pride of place in the most stunning locations. Authenticity and exceptional service are baked into the brand and are incomparable across the travel industry. As it continues to grow, a best-in-class online experience is a must.

So how do we stay relevant?

How can we stay on top of our game?

What are the silver bullets that connect with their targets within this utterly fragmented world? The answer is not the mediums, but the messages—the content of the work we create.

After two decades, we have learned some very valuable lessons:

1. Our people are our most prized asset; though team building, chemistry and talent may be difficult to cultivate, they yield the greatest return.*

2. Our business is built upon relationships—they are essential to our success and consistently bring opportunity our way while invariably opening new doors.

3. We never allow ourselves to become complacent, because the moment you do, the rug gets pulled from under you.

4. We don't believe any press we get—good or bad.

5. We treat every piece of new business as if it's our best and last.

6. Without the trust of our clients and their belief in our potential, our achievements would not be possible.

7. When contemplating the value of the message versus the medium, we choose the message—the medium has a short shelf life.

8. Since consumers don't attend our meetings, read our memos or review our strategy decks, each deliverable must be fully self-explanatory, informative, distinctive, engaging and memorable.

9. Work that is tasteful, well-crafted and witty will endure.

This book commemorates our 20th year in business. Rather than bore everyone with case studies or deep dives into work histories with esoteric narratives, we sifted through thousands of projects—without preference for any product, chronology or medium—and simply organized them by color (because that was what made the most sense).

The only common thread between them is their exemplary (we think) level of taste, craft and wit—the essence of what makes And Partners...us.

DAVID SCHIMMEL

*We have always been fortunate to work with extraordinary designers, typographers, photographers, illustrators, artists, directors, producers, writers and strategists. Without them, the pages of this book would not be as replete with such high-caliber work.

Work in progress documenting the making of this book, which involved poring over thousands of images and transparencies from the firm's archives to identify logical color/image pairings

The Full Spectrum

52   98   114   138   172

f Taste, Craft & Wit

204   218   228   252   268

"Bad taste is simply saying the truth before it should be said."

MEL BROOKS

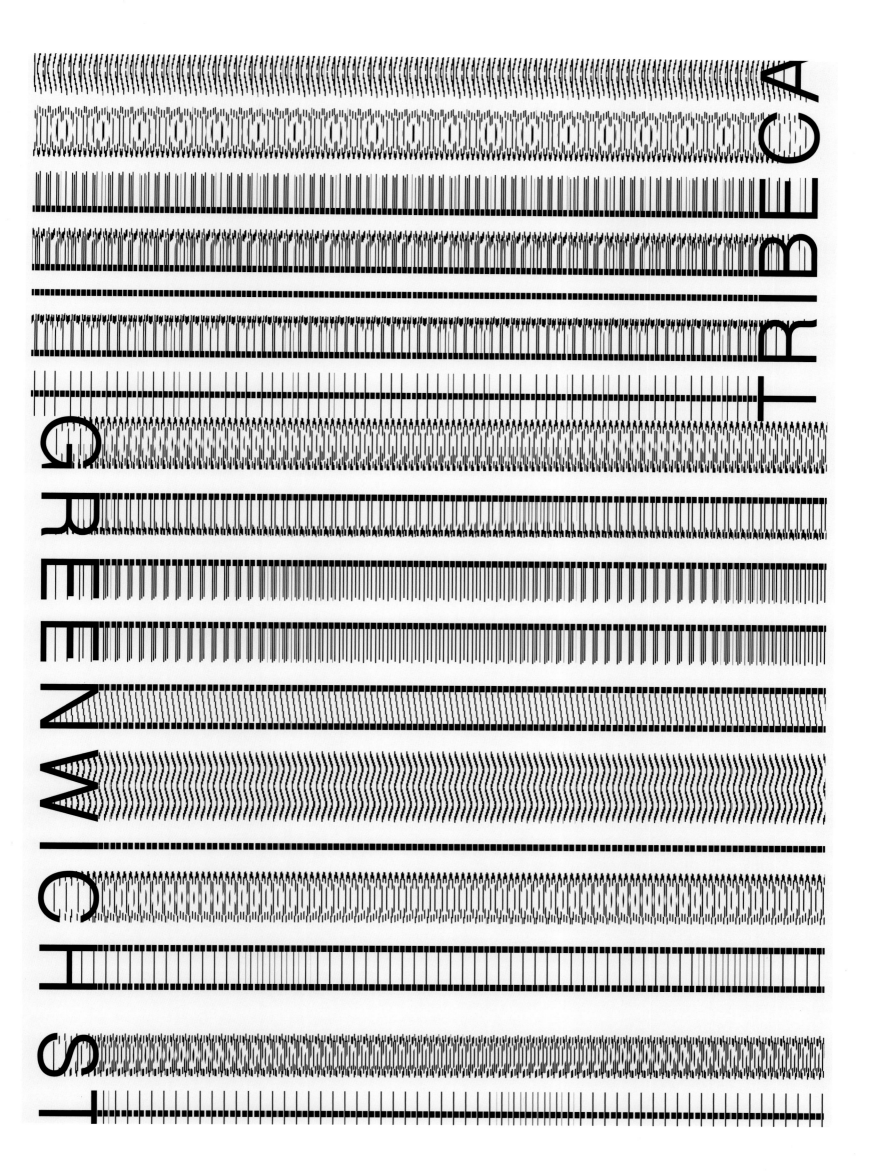

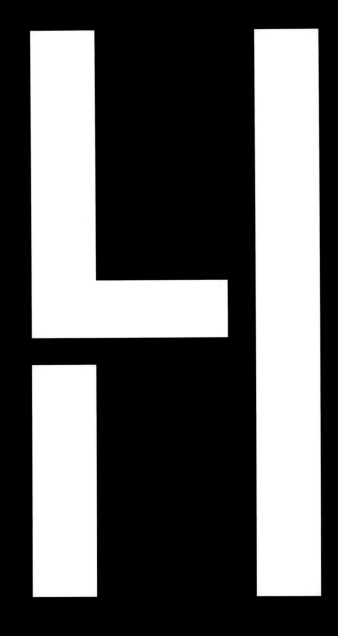

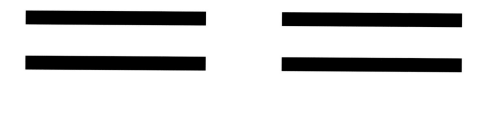

LIKE NO OTHER

LIKE NO OTHER

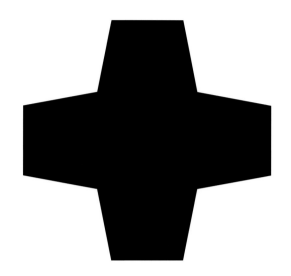

•Hub

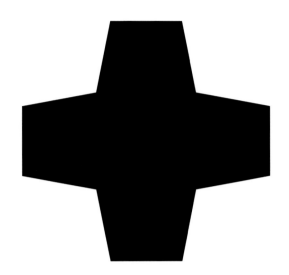

•Hub

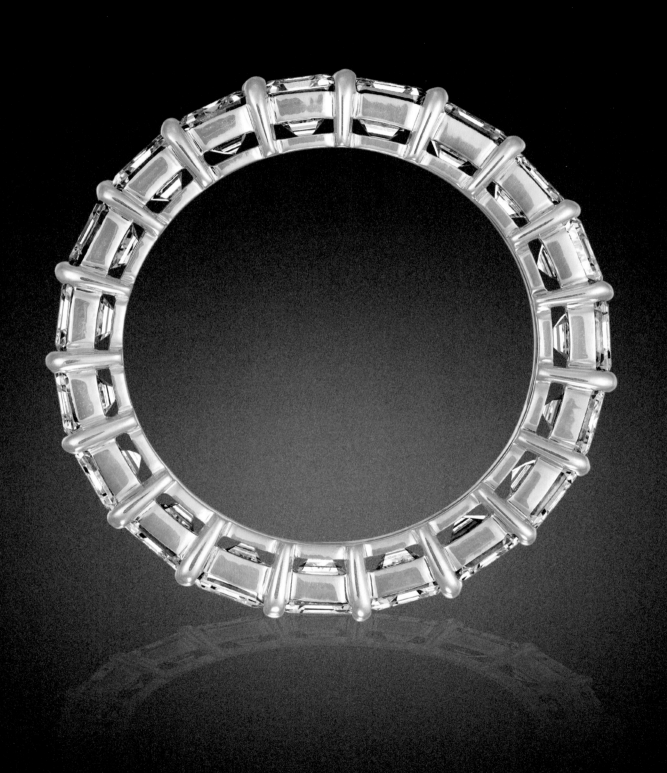

L
O V
E M I
G H T B E
B L I N D

BUT SHE'S NOT

L
LEO INGWER
EST. 1939

VALLEJO ST

POLK STREET

BROADWAY

LORD STANLEY ●

CHEESE PLUS ●

PACIFIC AVE

CRAFTSMAN AND WOLVES ●

● BELCAMPO MEAT CO.

JACKSON ST

CROSSFIT GOLDEN GATE ●

● WAGS

ST. LIGHTNING ●

HOUSE OF PRIME RIB ●

WASHINGTON ST

THE CREPE HOUSE ●

● 1760

CINCH SALOON ●

● AMELIE

CLAY ST

HARPER & RYE ●

CO NAM ●

BOB'S DONUTS ●

ACQUERELLO ●

● RANGOON RUBY BURMESE CUISINE

SACRAMENTO ST

SWAN OYSTER DEPOT ●

PLANT WAREHOUSE ●

● MARINE LAYER ● MYMY COFFEE SHOP ● OLEA CALIFORNIA ST

WHOLE FOODS MARKET ●

HI-LO CLUB ●

● TRADER JOE'S

SHALIMAR ●

1512 BARBER SHOP ●

SPINNERIE ●

PINE STREET

THE GRUBSTAKE ●

THE AUSTIN

BATTER BAKERY ●

● BIKRAM YOGA NOB HILL

AUSTIN ST

OCTAVIA ●

BUSH ST

PEOPLES BARBER & SHOP ●

FERN ALLEY

STR/KE MVMNT ●

● R BAR

SUTTER ST

● LOUIE'S GEN-GEN ROOM ● LIHOLIHO YACHT CLUB

● MR. HOLMES BAKEHOUSE

POST ST

● JANE GEARY ST

AMC VAN NESS ●

PLANT WAREHOUSE
1624 California Street
San Francisco, CA 94109
415.885.1515

ST. LIGHTNING
1813 Polk Street
San Francisco, CA 94109
415.400.4579

STR/KE MVMNT
1215 Polk Street
San Francisco, CA 94109
628.444.3166

THE POUR HOUSE
1327 Polk St
San Francisco, CA 94109
415.440.7662
sfpourhouse.com

UPCIDER
1160 Polk St
San Francisco, CA 94109
415.577.5205
upcidersf.com

SHALIMAR
1409 Polk Street
San Francisco, CA 94109
415.776.4642
shalimarsf.com

SPINNERIE
1401 Polk Street
San Francisco, CA 94109
415.345.1999
spinnerie.com

...rancisco, CA 94109
415.610.4333
rangoonruby.com

415.567.5432
acquerello.com

BELCAMPO MEAT CO.
1998 Polk Street
San Francisco, CA 94109
415.660.5573
belcampo.com

BOB'S DONUTS
1621 Polk Street
San Francisco, CA 94109
415.776.3141
bobsdonutsf.com

ABCDE
FGHIJKL
MNOPQ
RSTUVW
XYZ

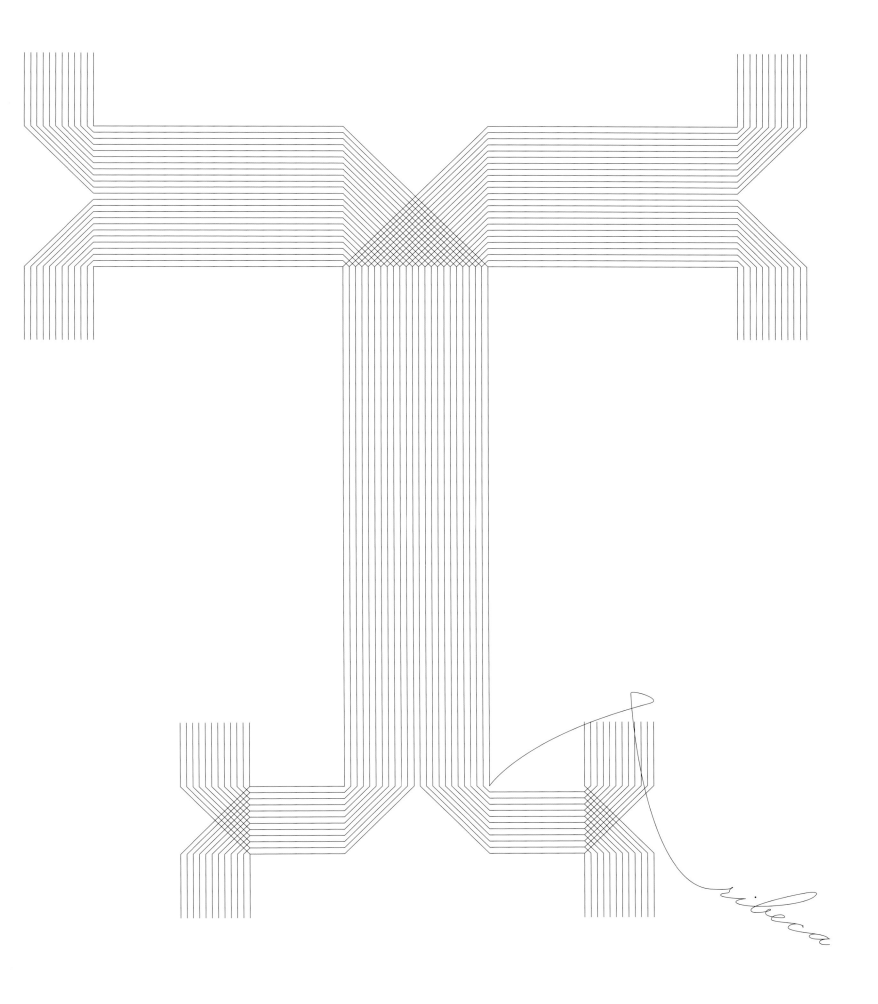

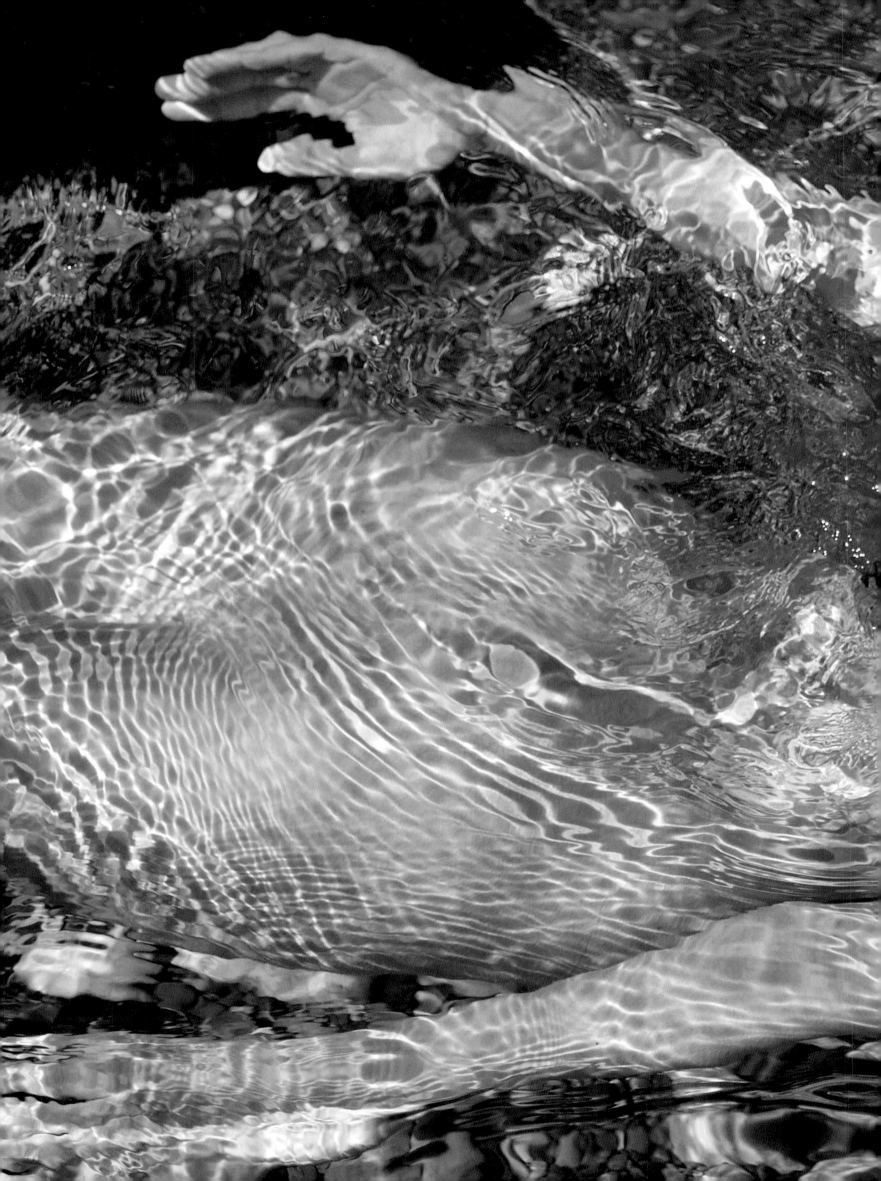

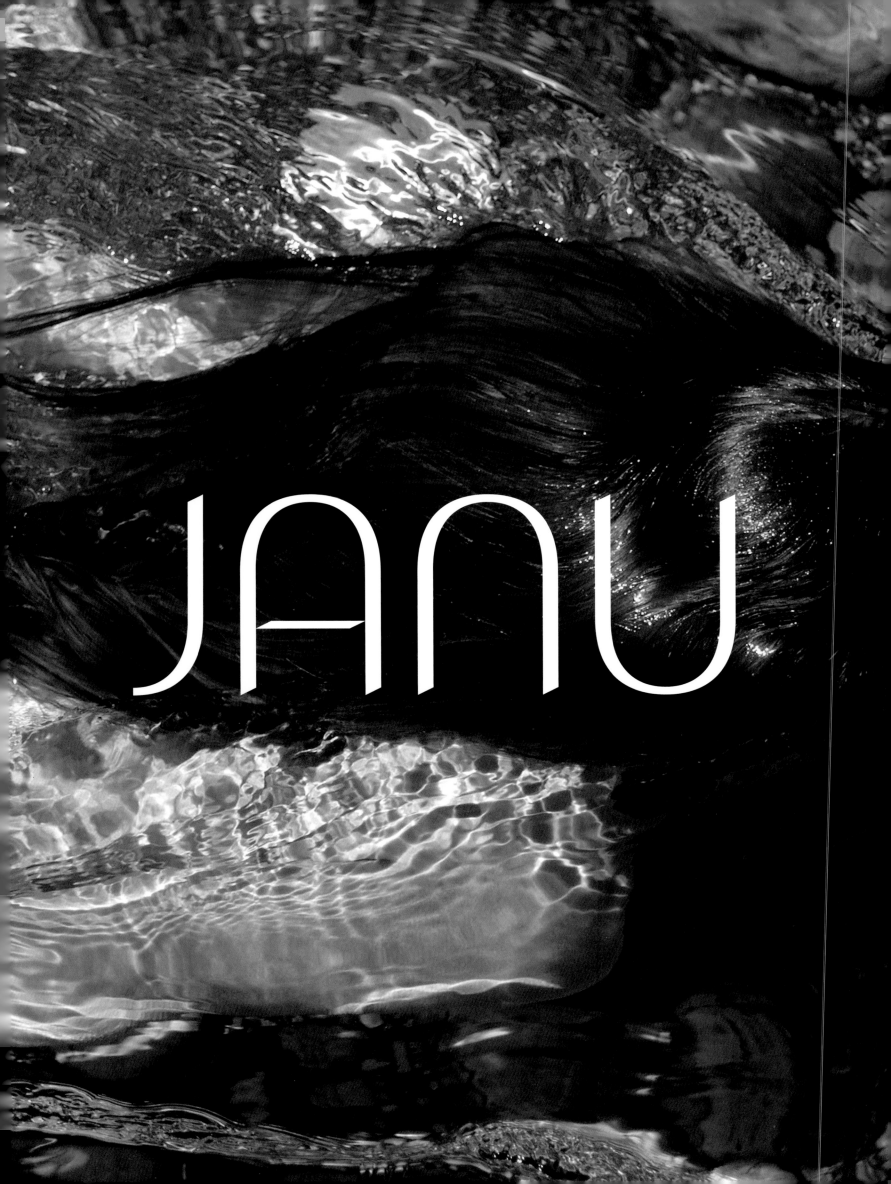

JANU MONTENEGRO

RETHINK BALANCE

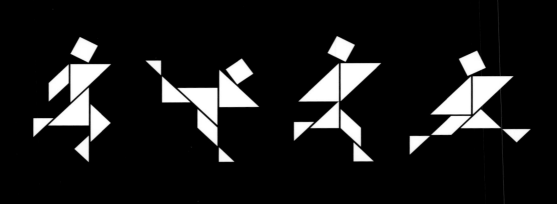

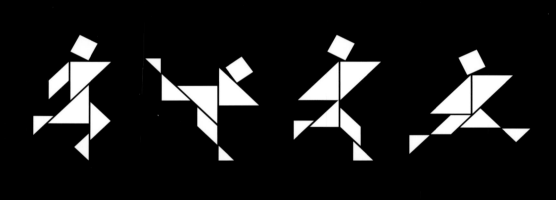

this
read
raise
money
facts
license
bits
seen

that
write
promote
time
figures
registration
bytes
noted

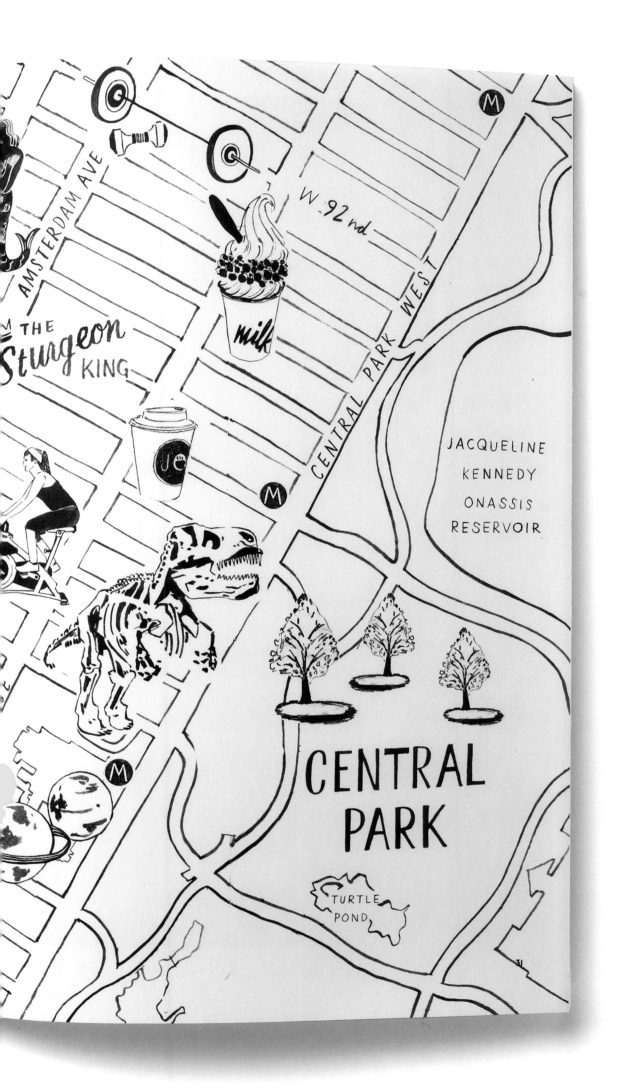

AMSTERDAM AVE

THE Sturgeon KING

milk

je

W. 92 nd

CENTRAL PARK WEST

M

M

M

JACQUELINE
KENNEDY
ONASSIS
RESERVOIR

CENTRAL
PARK

TURTLE
POND

CHATSWORTH

344 WEST 72

"Change is inevitable, and when it happens, the wisest response is not to wail or whine but to suck it up and deal with it."

DANIEL H. PINK

SAVE / RETRIEVE
PERSONAL
AND EDUCATION
RELATED
INFORMATION

AN EDUCATION AND
COMMUNITY BASED
NETWORK FOR EVERYONE

COMMUNICATE AND
COLLABORATE ONLINE

CHAT

FROM
ERE
NTERNET
CTION

PRO

BE

YOUR
WORK
AVAILABLE
AT HOME

ONLINE

NOW

Which
comes
first,
knowledge
or
experience?

specLogix

GLEN COVE

Co

Commercial

Park

Park

Anglers Club

Ferry Terminal

Anglers Marina

Playgrou

N

E

261 HUDSON

66 The ultimate freedom for creative groups is the freedom to experiment with new ideas. Some skeptics insist that innovation is expensive. In the long run, innovation is cheap. Mediocrity is expensive—and autonomy can be the antidote. 99

TOM KELLEY, IDEO

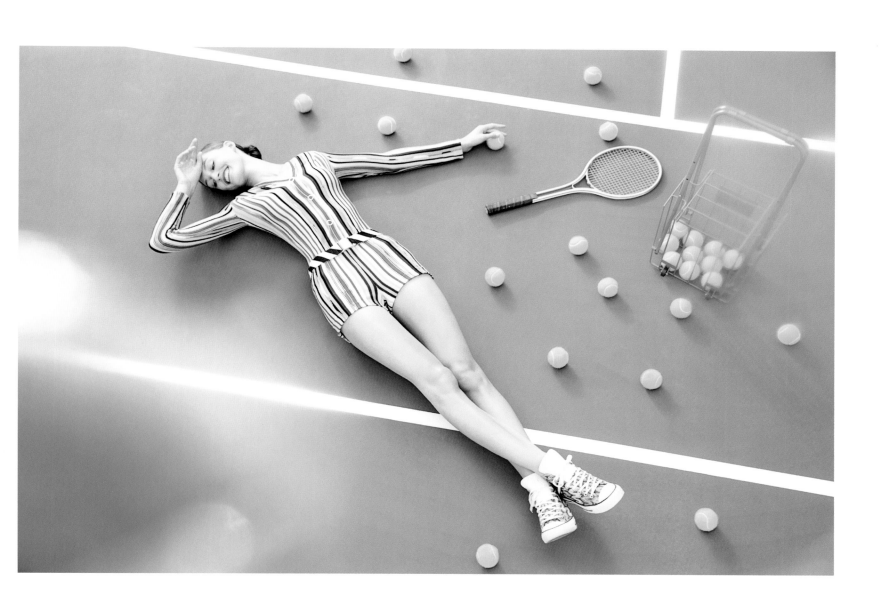

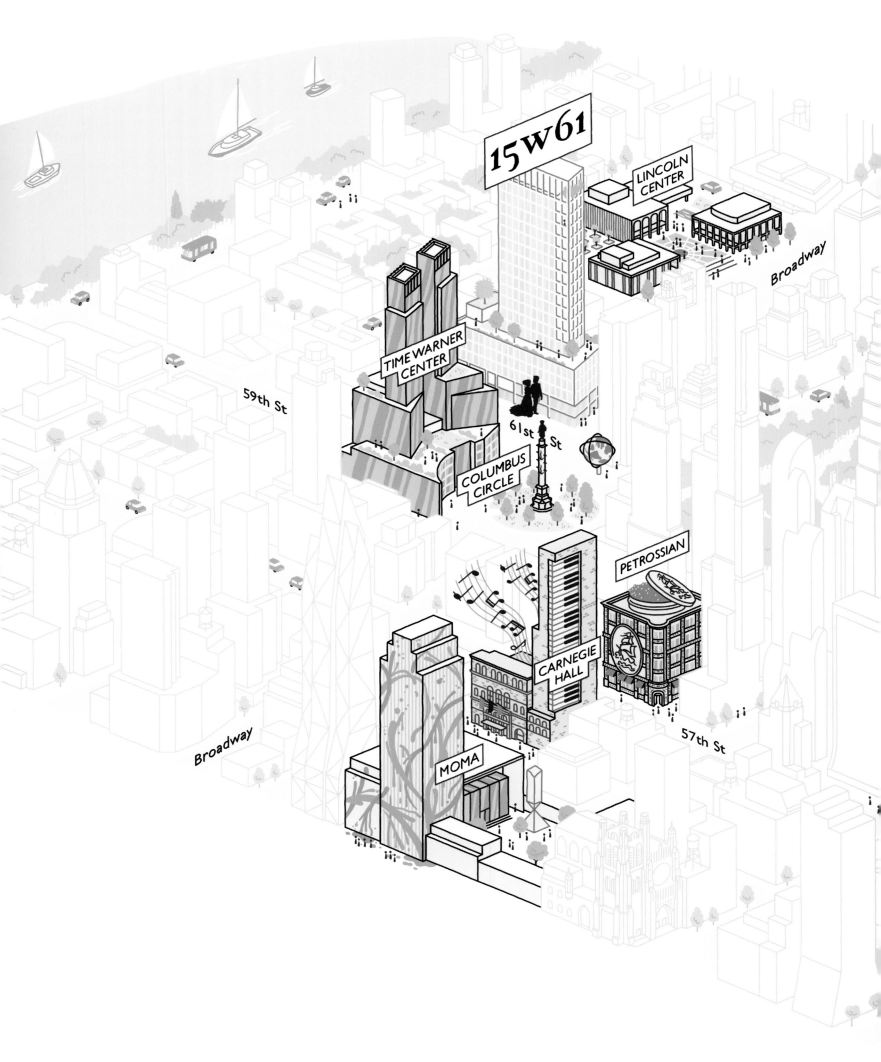

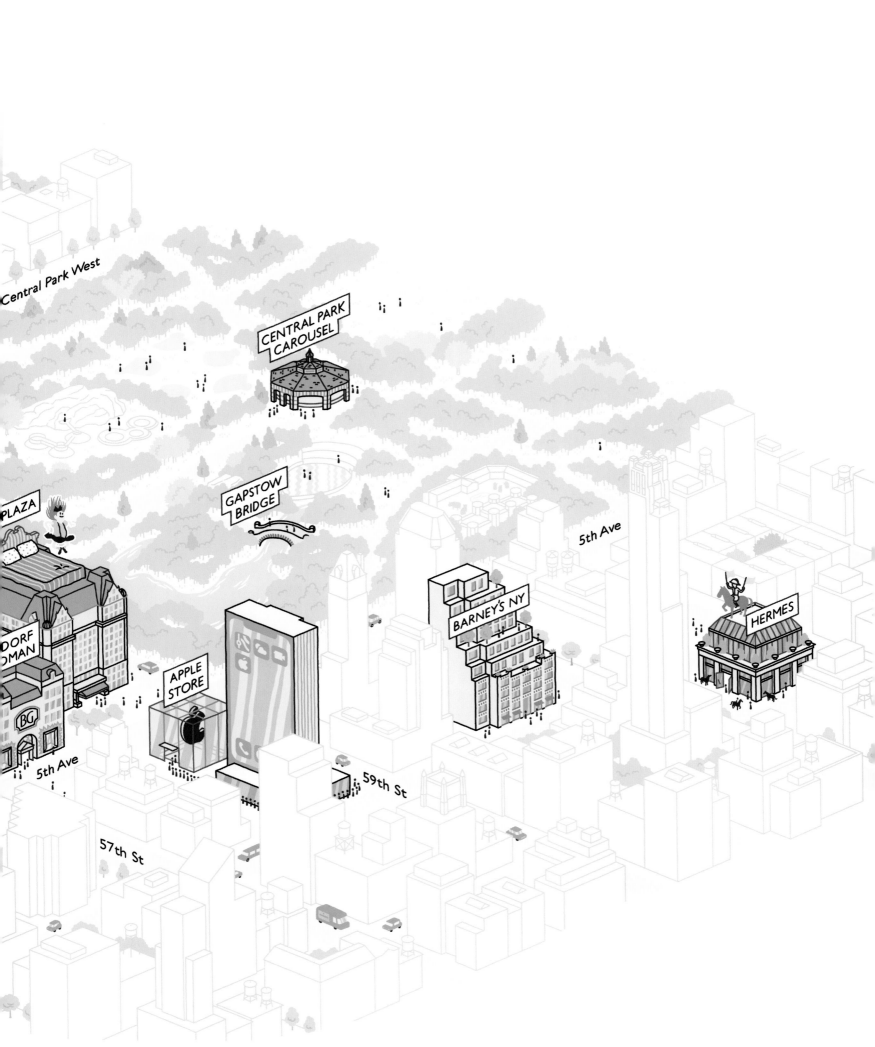

JACKSON PARK

PLAY BEAUTIFULLY

THIS IS THE SIDE THAT'S GREENEST

A PRIVATE PARK IS THE ULTIMATE AMENITY

Hello. Welcome to 1 Rector Park.

What's your 1 thing?

Set Price Range

$2.31M

Size

Choose Size

STUDIO 1BR 2BR 3BR 4BR

View

Selected Views

River View   Park View   Courtyard

View Availability List ▶

offering plan available from the sponsor. CD No. 08-0089
, LLC, 1114 Avenue of the Americas, New York, NY 10036.   *corcoran sunshine*   ©2010, 1 Rector Park
333 Rector Place, New York, NY 10280

Hello, I'm _____, email me at _____

name*   email*

or call my cell, _____. I'm interes

phone number

_____ for about _____

residence type*   price range*

move around _____. I found H

calendar

_____, and look forward to hearing

how did you hear about us?

soon.

required fields*

submit

ABCDEFG
OPQRSTU
1234567

HIJKLMN
VWXYZ
890

Dior by Avedon

66 Let me tell you one thing. In the world we live in, 98 percent of what gets built and designed today is pure shit. 99

FRANK GEHRY

olivia@missonibaia.com
+1 786 303 0033

777 N.E. 26 Terrace, Miami, FL
+1 305 800 7000   missonibai

MISSONIbaia

Olivia Seovac
Senior Sales Executive

CAVA

MA

GRACE

Brookfield
Properties

LLERI
BU

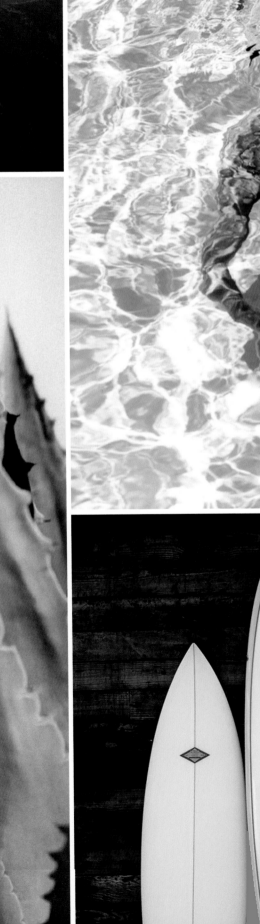

THE BUILDING floor-to-ceiling glass curtain wall / open views of the Manhattan streetscape / argon gas-filled windows for superior sound attenuation / **AMENITIES + FEATURES** full-time doorman and concierge / on-site resident manager / roof terrace with outdoor dining and adjoining indoor lounge / library with fireplace / game room / media room / dining room with adjoining pantry / golf simulator / indoor pool / fitness center with high-performance equipment / locker rooms / half-court basketball / yoga studio / spin studio / **KITCHENS** custom cabinetry with polished chrome pulls / under-cabinet lighting / polished quartz countertops / Liebherr paneled refrigerator / Bertazzoni natural-gas cooktop and speed oven / Blomberg paneled dishwasher / Aggio hood / staggered pencil-tile and glass backsplash / exceptional storage / **BATHROOMS** elegant floor-to-ceiling tile creates a natural stone look / walk-in shower or bathtub / custom wood vanity / Kohler commode / Hansgrohe fixtures in polished nickel ◦

GRACE

Brookfield
Properties

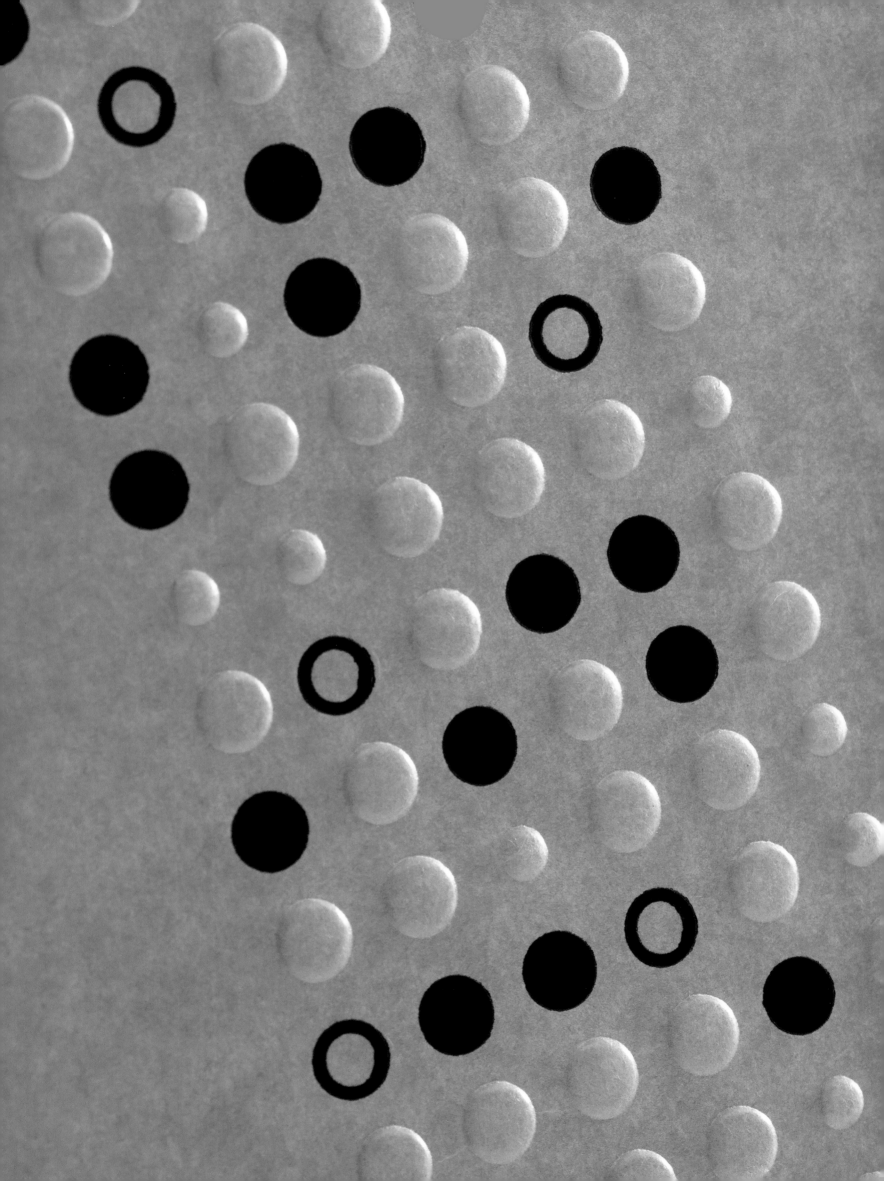

RIVERBANK

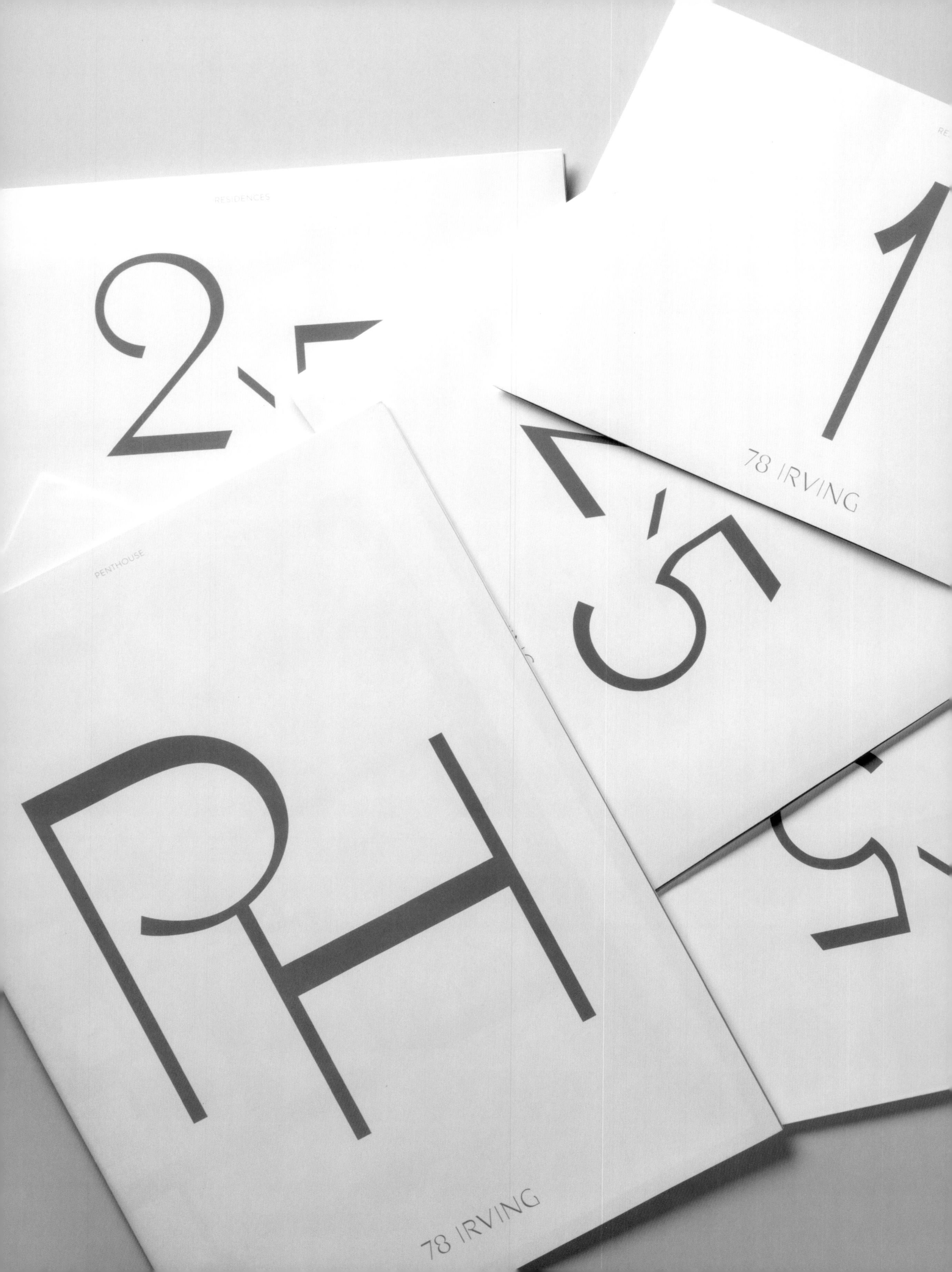
RESIDENCES
2
1
78 IRVING
PENTHOUSE
PH
78 IRVING

ly into three great classes, according to the attitude they hold to life

ld to see how much they can get out of it. Provided they are comfortabl

to get all they can and to keep all they get, it sometimes seems a matter o

The people of this class are often rich, sometimes they are talented; but

s. They never find the contentment and happiness they seek so eagerly. Th

ke to think very deeply of anything. They are contented to drift along an

y are often well-meaning, amiable people; but if all the people in the worl

standstill. The people of the third class believe that they are in the worl

willing to give up their lives to the selfish pursuit of pleasure. They believ

problems of life, but meet and solve them. It is to these that the world

for all hope of progress in the future. The people who belong to this cla

piest people in the world. Now, if you want to belong to one of the fir

ys to be selfish or lazy. You would not be in the spirit of the school if yo

the fun you are going to have – the hunting, fishing, and cruising – and

truth, and purity, and helpfulness – you would only be a hindrance to u

pleasures of the outdoor life we try to give our boys, we believe more i

ur wish to belong to the third class – to live not for yourself alone, but t

trength – why then, my boy, this will be a good place for you and we wi

, you will not find it difficult to commit yourself to the promises that I as

If you wish to become an efficient, helpful, trustworthy ma

accustom yourself to obey, to work and to resist self-indulgence. As th

one day before deciding. If you then decide that you want to come to u

envelope that I enclose for that purpose. Of the two other copies, one

henever you feel inclined to do so, and thus refresh your memory of wha

en into your confidence in a matter of so much importance as this. If yo

so frankly, enclosing your letter in the addressed envelope, and we will l

rinted that it is something that is a mere matter of form. Though it is se

xpressly to you personally. It comes directly from my heart to yours, and

If you sign the answering letter I want you to feel that as long as you a

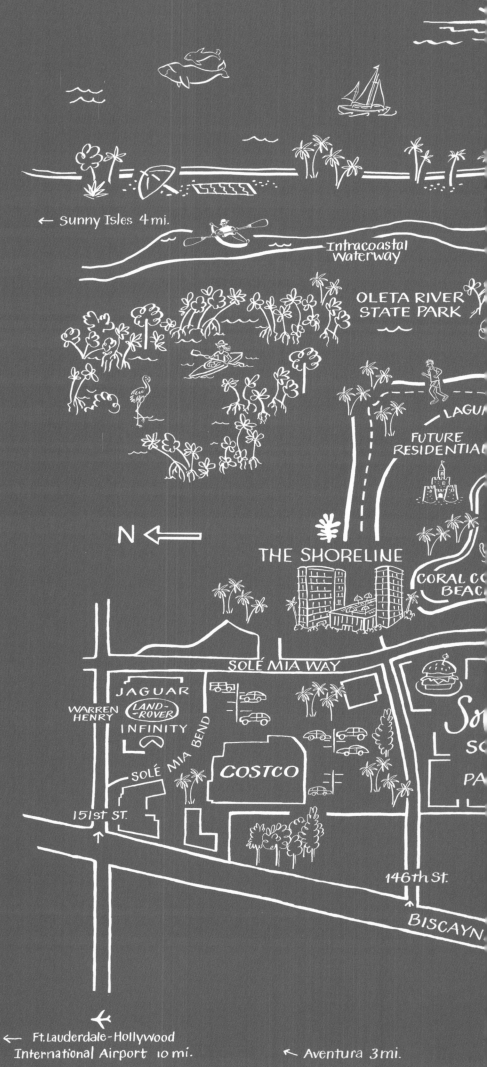

← Sunny Isles 4 mi.

Intracoastal Waterway

OLETA RIVER STATE PARK

LAGU...

FUTURE RESIDENTIA...

N ←

THE SHORELINE

CORAL C... BEACH...

SOLÉ MIA WAY

JAGUAR

LAND-ROVER

WARREN HENRY

INFINITY

SOLÉ MIA BEND

So...

SO...

PA...

COSTCO

151st ST.

146th ST.

BISCAYN...

← Ft. Lauderdale-Hollywood International Airport 10 mi.

← Aventura 3 mi.

Atlantic
Ocean

HAULOVER PARK   Bal Harbour 4.5 mi. →

FIU
BISCAYNE BAY CAMPUS

SOLÉ
BEACH
CLUB

FUTURE
RESIDENTIAL

FUTURE
RESIDENTIAL

TEL

SOLÉ MIA WAY

FUTURE
SCHOOL

SOLÉ MIA LANE

143rd St.

U.S. 1

138th St.

FUTURE
PARK

iami Beach 11 mi. →
wntown Miami 11 mi. →

Miami
International Airport 9 mi. ↘

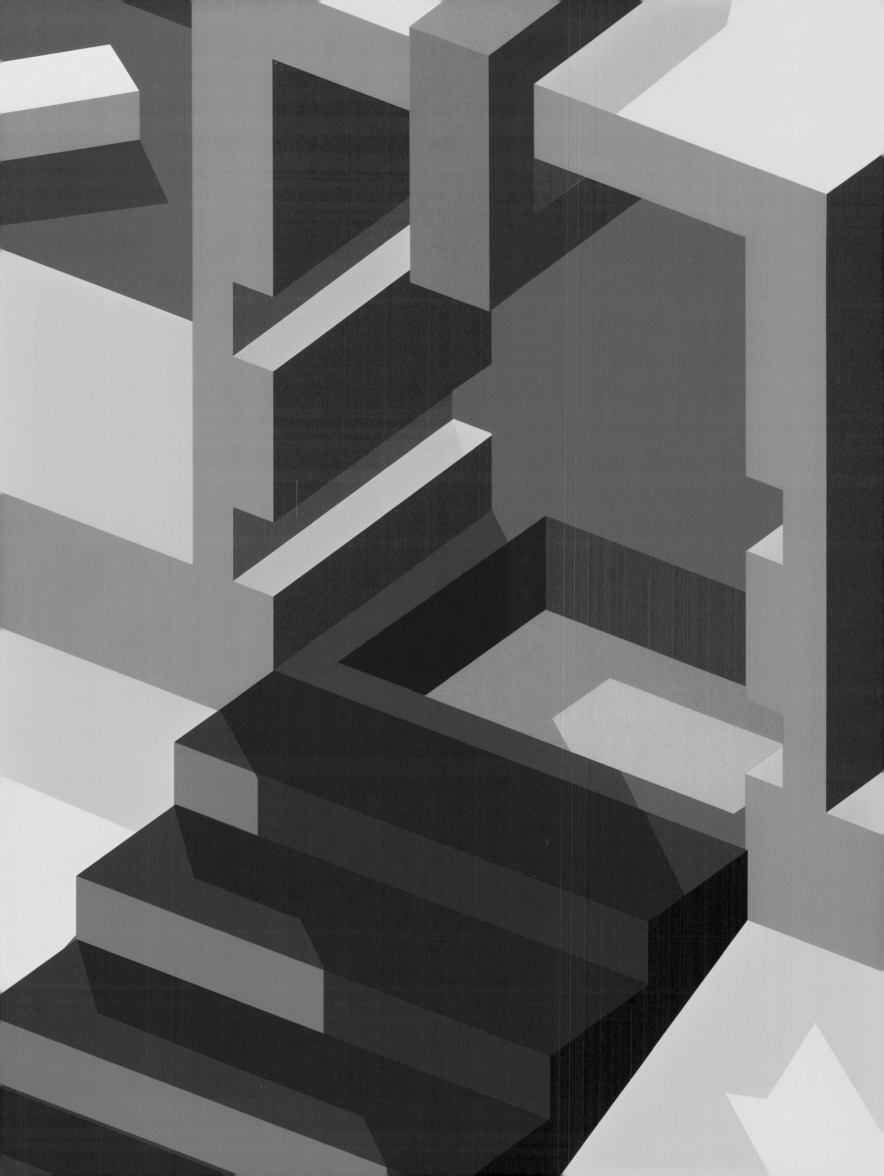

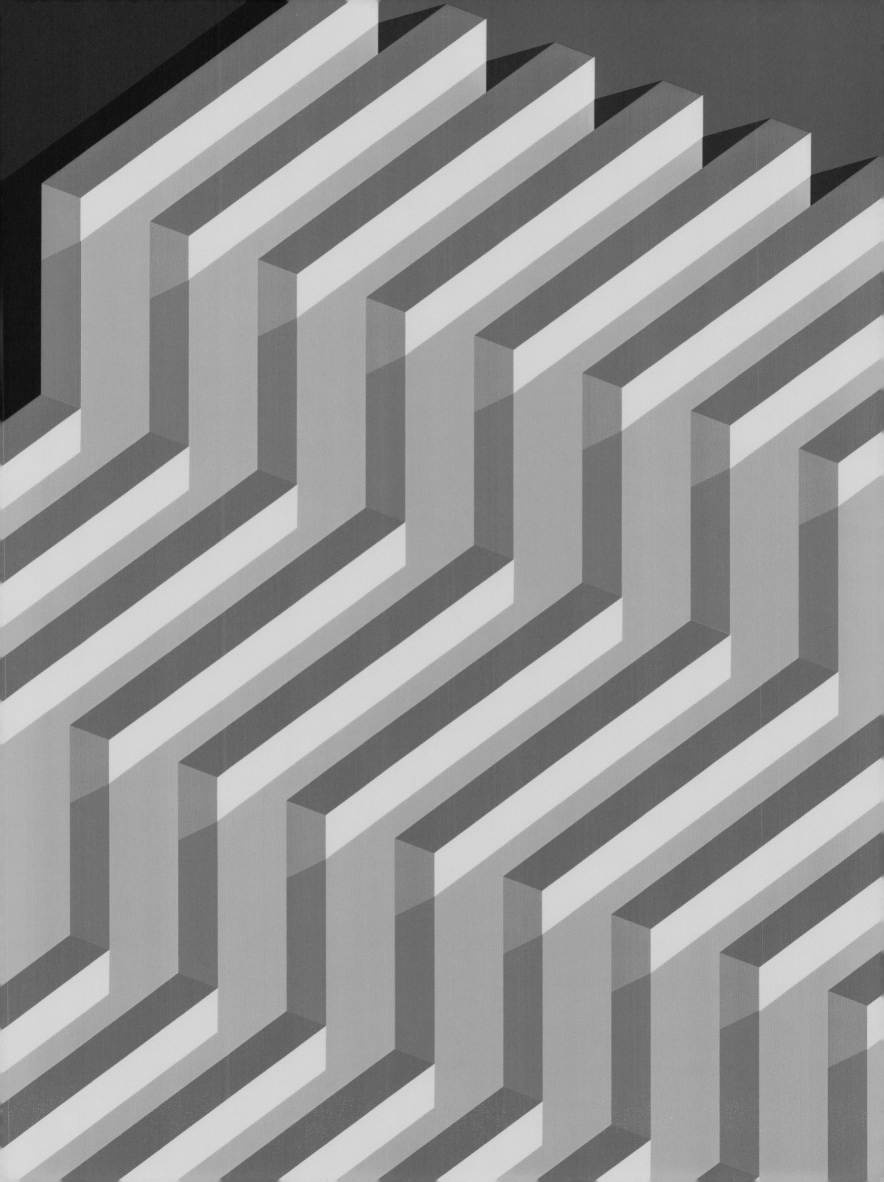

> **"Good design is a Renaissance attitude that combines technology, cognitive science, human need and beauty to produce something that the world didn't know it was missing."**

PAOLA ANTONELLI
Senior Curator of Architecture and Design,
Museum of Modern Art

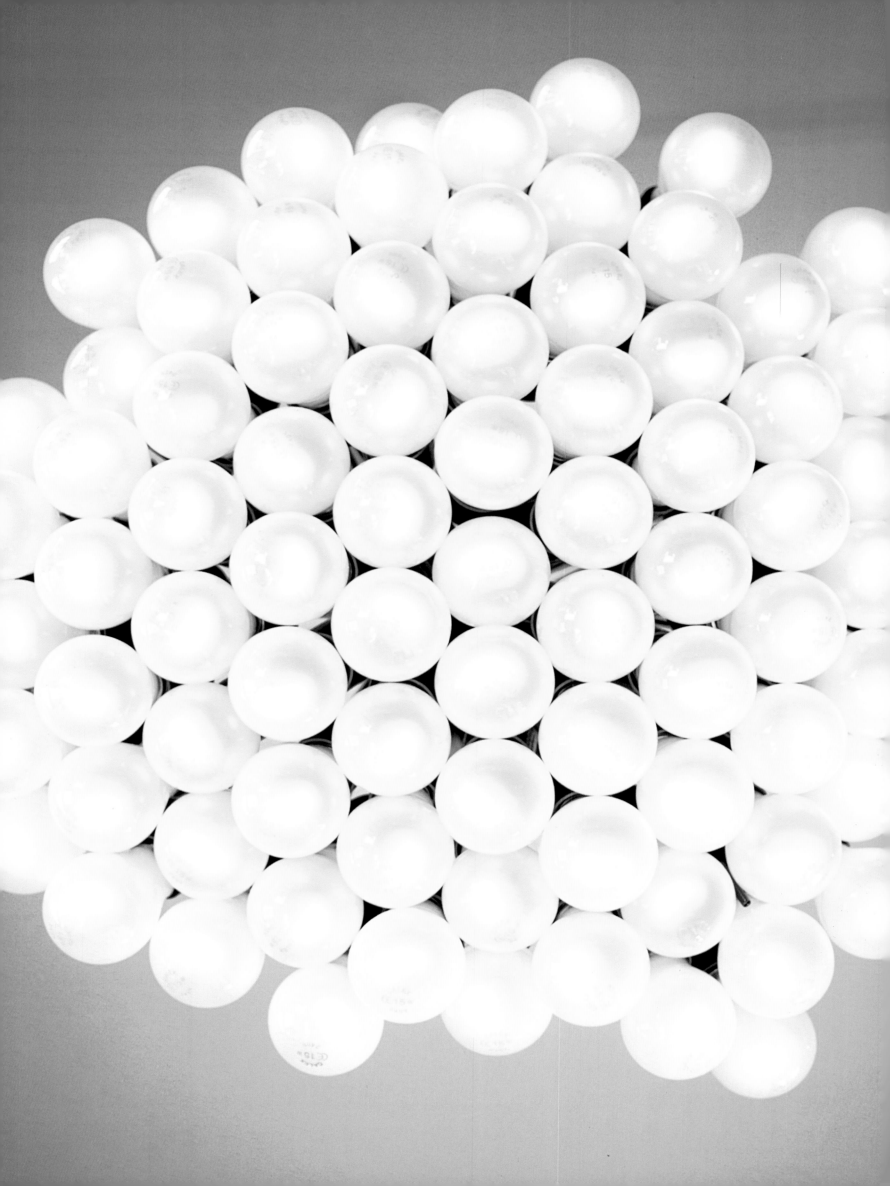

GREAT JONES ALLEY

Bank
with
Interesting.

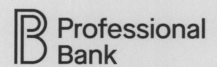
Professional
Bank

RETHINK BALANCE

JANU

MONTENEGRO

BRIGHT IDEAS BECOME BRILLIANT REALITY
WITH CLASSIC® BRAND PAPERS

NEENAH PAPER

1/2
the job

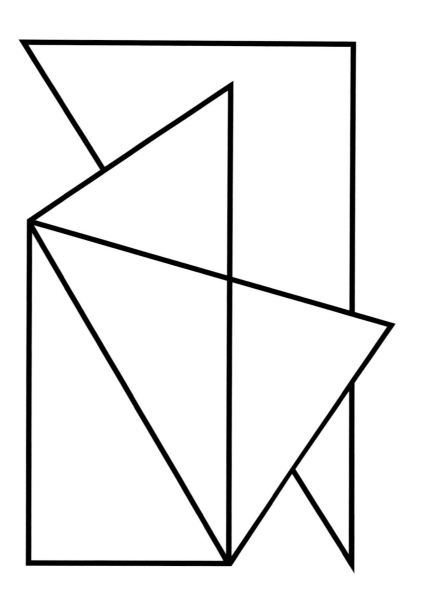

ONE BENNETT PARK

ONE BENNETT PARK

SALES SUITE: 350 W. HUBBARD STREET, SUITE 300 CHICAGO, IL 60654 · 312 662 1900 · ONEBENNETTPARK.COM

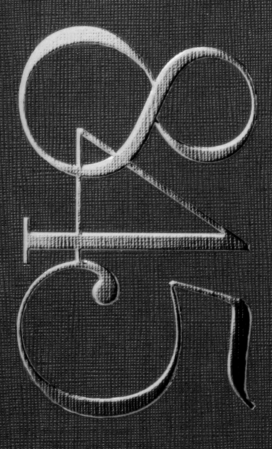

WEST END

avenue

FIND YOUR VOICE. IT'S
AND FIGHT BACK. ON
THE SUPREME COURT
CONSTITUTIONAL RIGHT
IN ITS LANDMARK *ROE*
TODAY THIS RIGHT IS
COURTROOMS ACROSS
CAN DO SOMETHING
ACTION TODAY, BEFORE

The President openly admires staunch anti-choice jurists
and is nominating extremists to the federal bench. Senators have
a constitutional duty to independently evaluate such nominees.
Yet, they have been pressured to rush their decision-making
and have, on occasion, been bypassed entirely.

THE EROSION OF FREEDOM IS A SLIPPERY SLOPE. IF WE LOSE REPRODUCTIVE RIGHTS, OTHER CORE RIGHTS—LIKE RELIGIOUS LIBERTY AND CIVIL RIGHTS—MAY BE CLOSE BEHIND.

THE FUTURE WILL BE SET BY JUDGES WHO HOLD LIFETIME SEATS ON THE FEDERAL BENCH. ANTI-CHOICE JUDGES ARE ALREADY ATTACKING THE RIGHT TO ABORTION. AND MORE ANTI-CHOICE NOMINEES ARE WAITING IN THE WINGS—POSITIONED TO RENDER DECISIONS THAT WILL DEFINE FREEDOM FOR GENERATIONS TO COME.

Laws restricting abortion pose serious risks to women.
In the two decades before abortion was legalized in the US, as many as
1.2 million women per year sought illegal "back alley" abortions.
Thousands died. Tens of thousands suffered serious medical injury.

Medically safe, legal abortion has had a profound effect
on the health and well being of American women. Today, abortion
is nearly twice as safe as a penicillin injection.

Within the visible collage fragment:

ound. Espec...
ng the viewer on her i
face, the layers benea
eflected in a mirror.
Henryson's work. Th
hide. Henryso
ey hide. bloo

AMANERA

RESORT OVERVIEW   >

CREATIVE TEAM   >

RESIDENCES   >

FLOOR PLANS   >

OWNING AT AMAN   >

GALLERY   >

🏠   HOME

END SESSION

AMANERA

66 The most basic way to get someone's attention is this: Break a pattern. 99

CHIP HEATH

VANS

CHANGE INC.

The Vans® brand is the original action sports and youth culture icon. But you can't stay original by doing what you've always done.

Almost 50 years ago, on the sun-soaked streets, sidewalks, stairs and empty swimming pools of Southern California, a brand and a movement were born at the same time. The *Vans*® brand and skateboarding grew up together. The brand's iconic, waffle-sole designed shoes, worn by the riders who created the sport, changed youth culture forever—impacting everything from film and music to art and fashion.

Skateboarding, and other action sports such as surfing, snowboarding and BMX, aren't like traditional sports. Although competition is one aspect of these sub-cultures, referees, rules and coaches are disliked by participants. Individuality reigns supreme. Drawing your own line and expressing yourself on your terms push these sports and their cultures forward.

These twin impulses of creative self-expression and individuality are universal. And they appeal to more than just athletes. They're for anyone who wants the freedom to be themselves—in their art, their music or their style. Among the young, who are most eager to make their unique mark on this world, these desires are amplified.

6
W I10 O
O

THE EASTON

205 EAST 92ND STREET

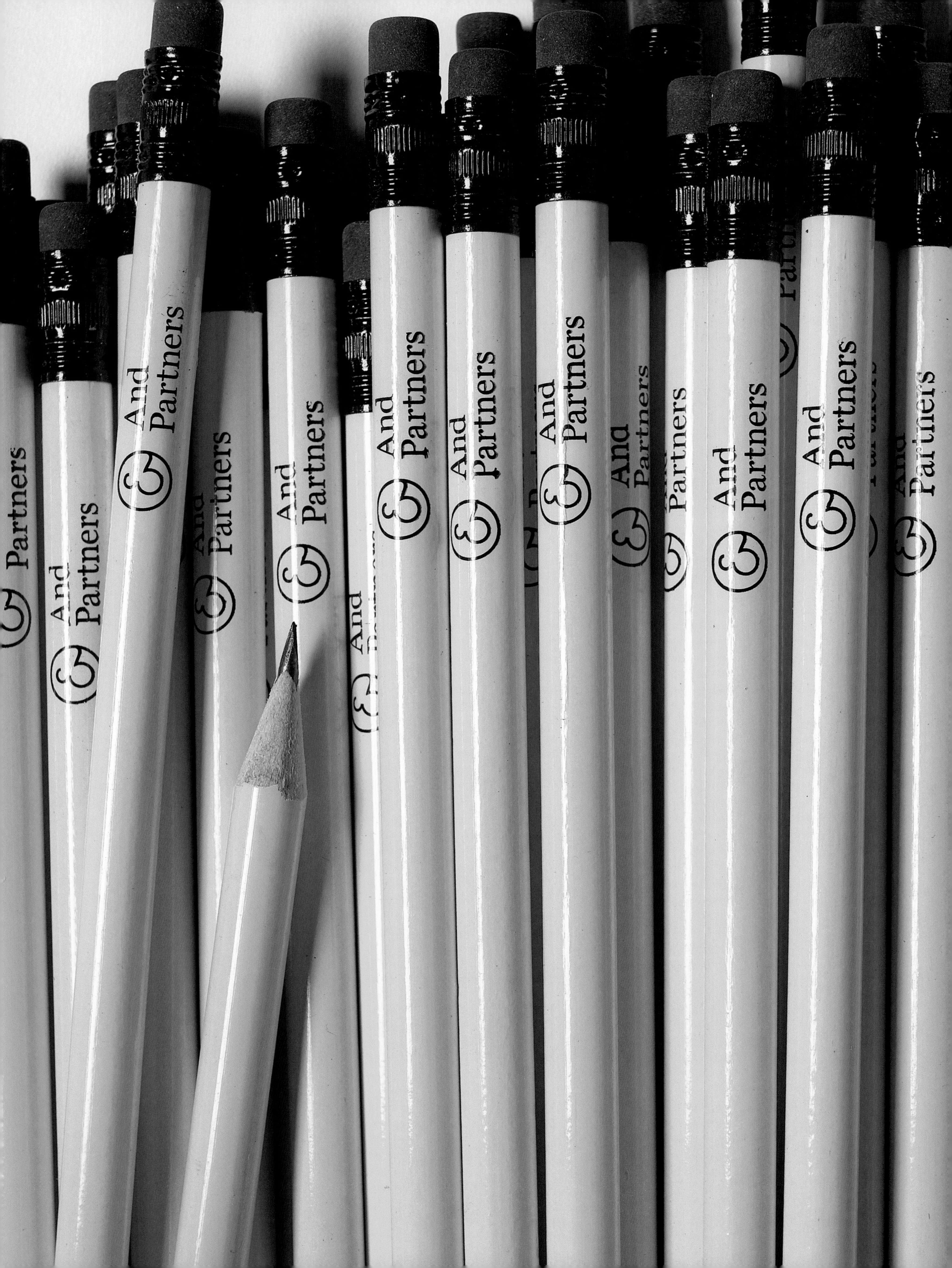
And
Partners

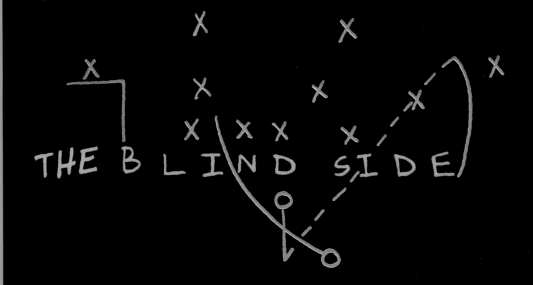

MICHAEL LEWIS

THE BLIND SIDE

EVOLUTION OF A GAME

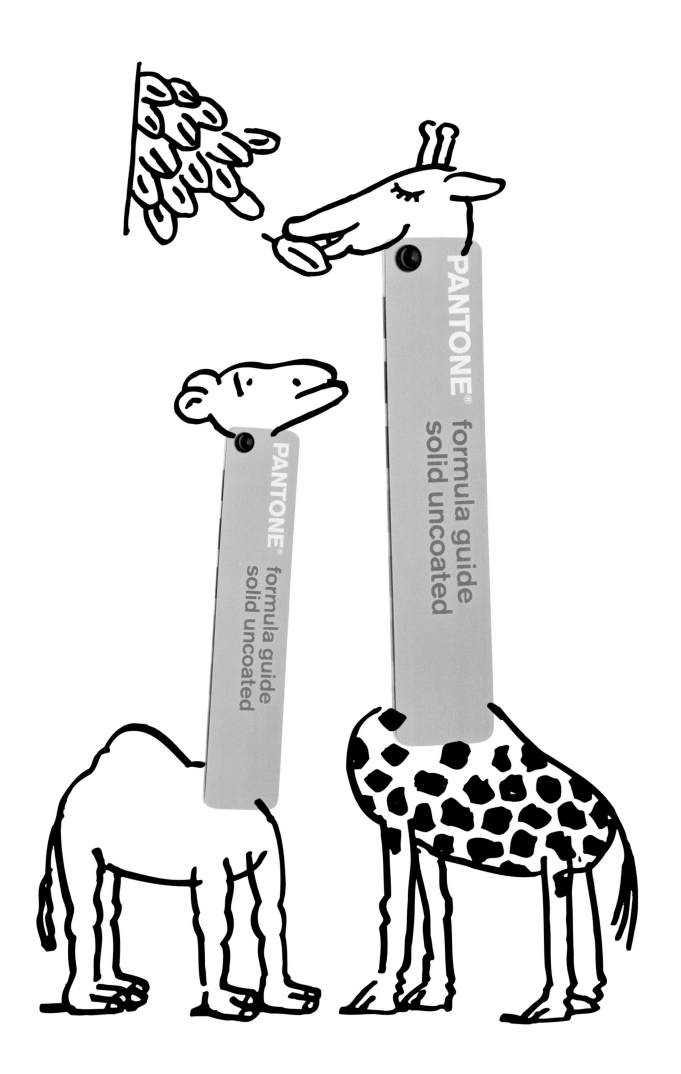

15 HUBERT

NEENAH PAPER

CLASSIC CREST® Papers
GIVE YOU MORE

110%

THE COMPLETE COMMUNICATOR

MISSONIbaia

"At the simplest level, only people who know they do not know everything will be curious enough to find things out."

VIRGINIA POSTREL

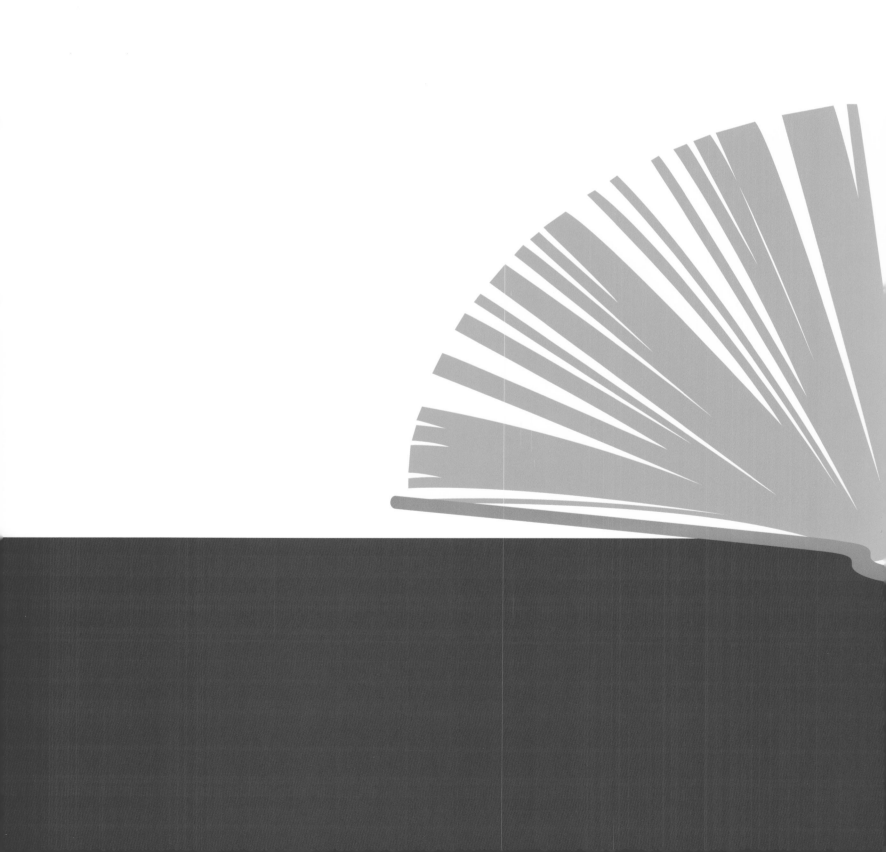

227

" **A foolish consistency is the hobgoblin of little minds.** "

RALPH WALDO EMERSON

and proven results

markets

nding

Delta Asset Management

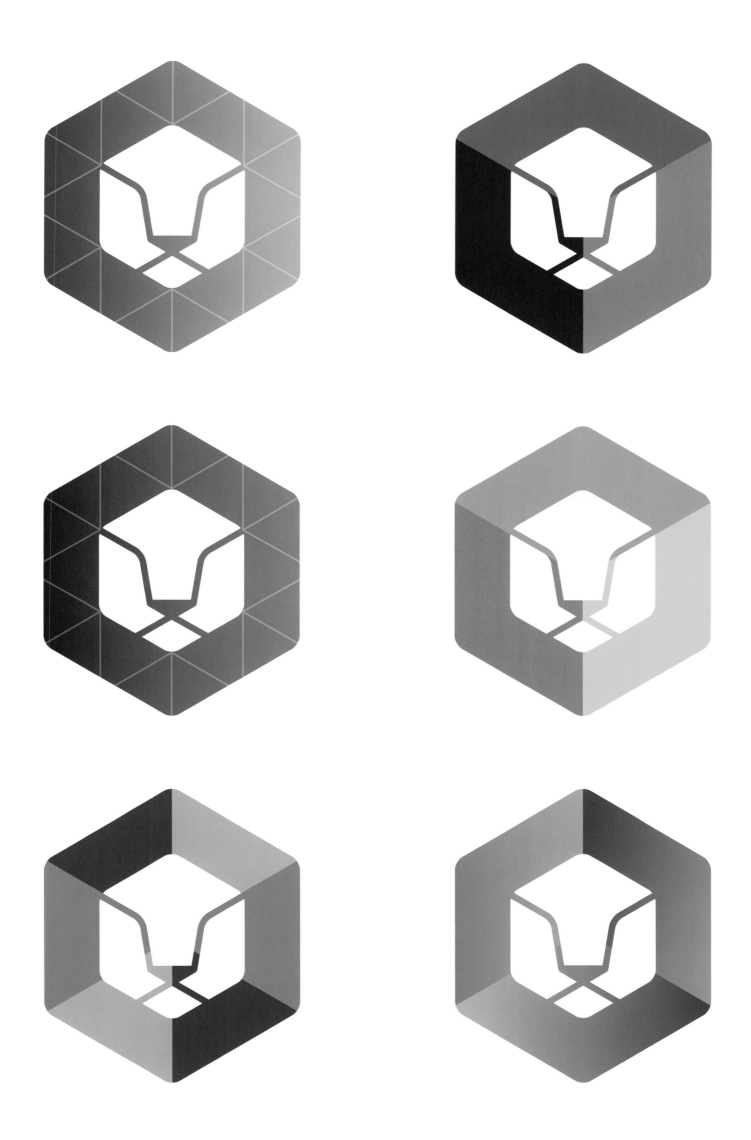

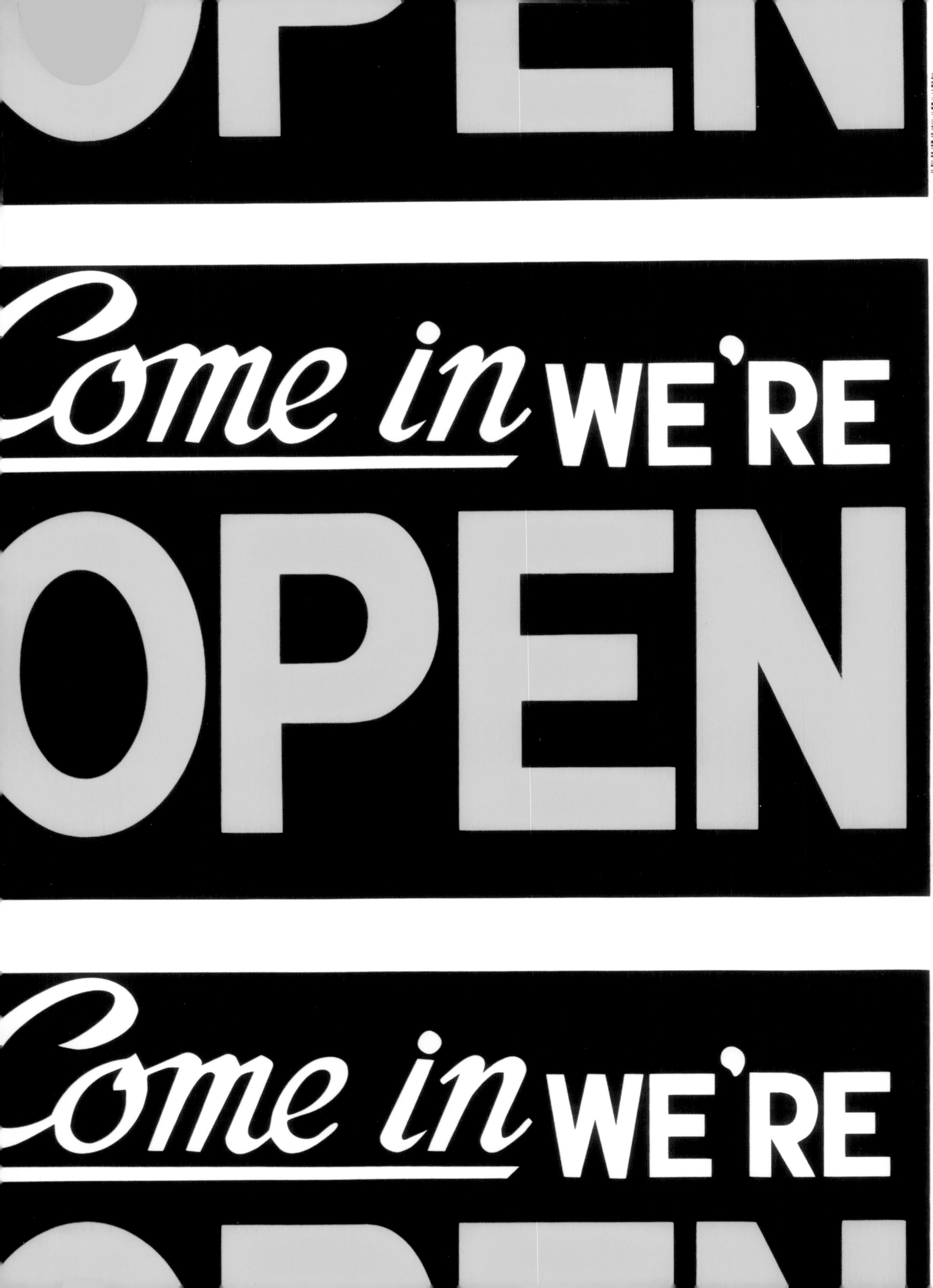
Come in WE'RE
OPEN
Come in WE'RE

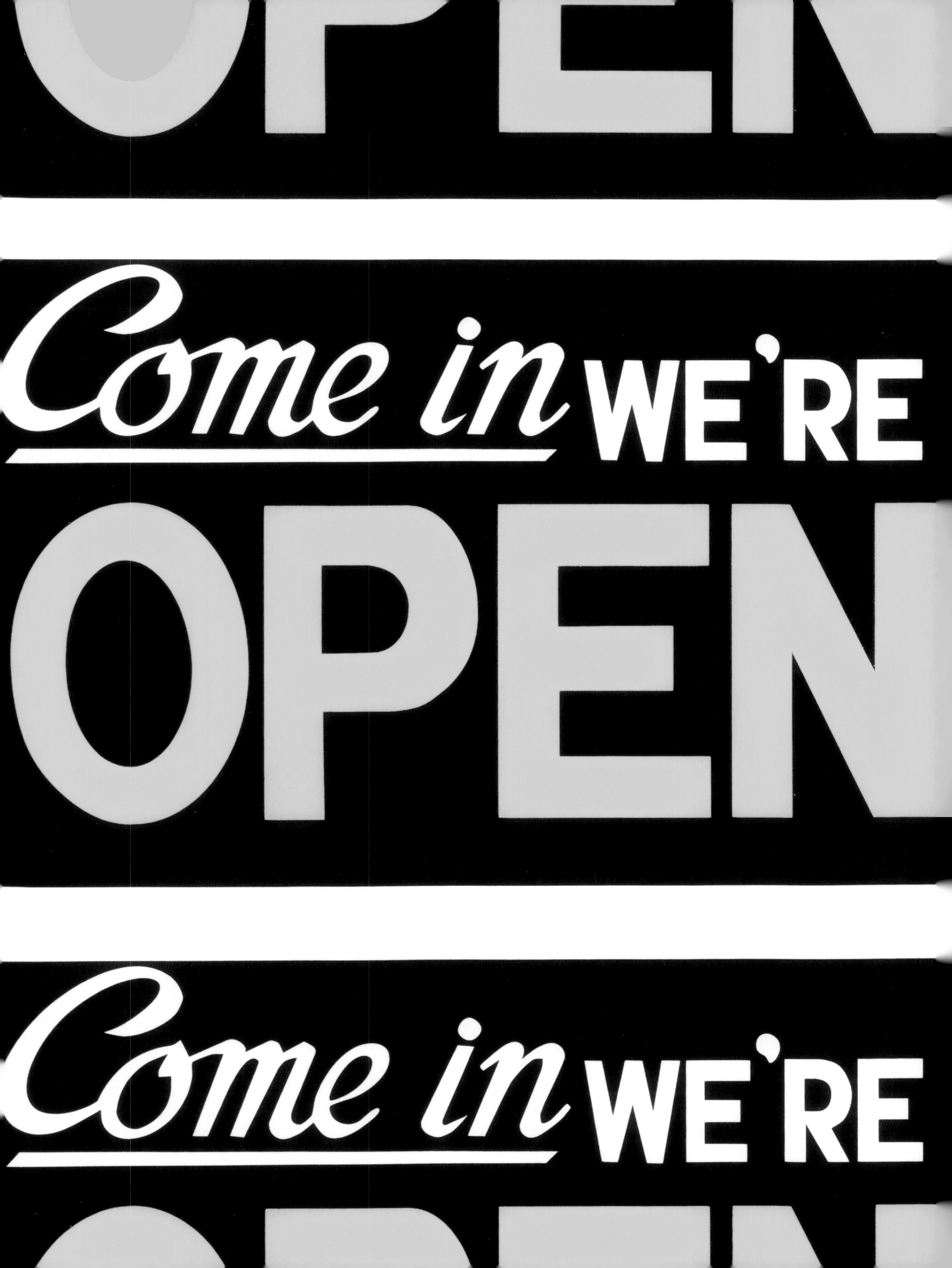

National Council of
Jewish Women

Summer 2007 vol. 30, no. 1

NCJ⋛®
JOURNAL

BUILDING BRIDGES, BRIDGING DIVIDES

Inside: The Cyber-Connection: Transforming Grassroots Activism
Are We There Yet? An Israeli Pioneer on the Gender Gap
Seven Things You Can Do to Build Bridges

Plus: Voting Matters, an *NCJW Journal* Series

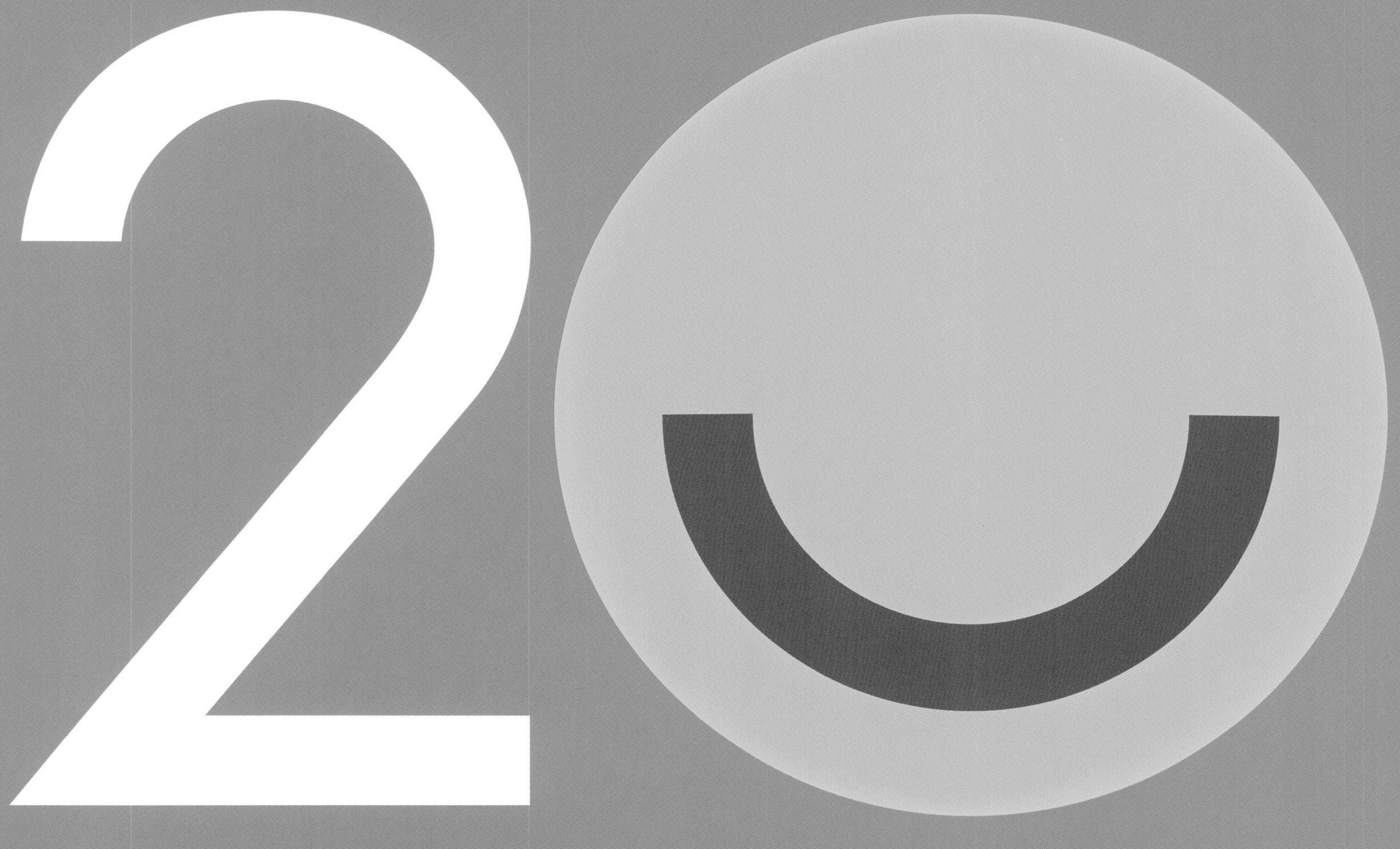
2

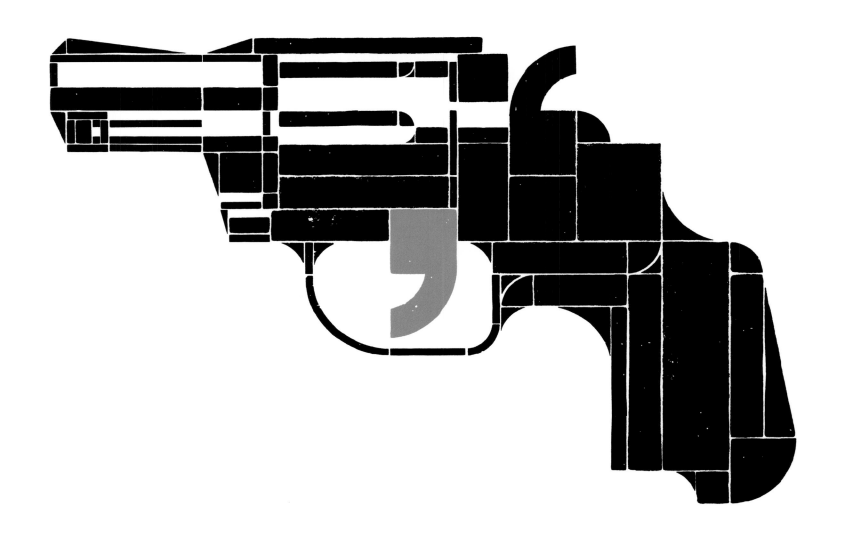

Paper Basics

Ask Mohawk

MICHAEL LEWIS

Moneyball

THE ART OF WINNING AN UNFAIR GAME

Peace.

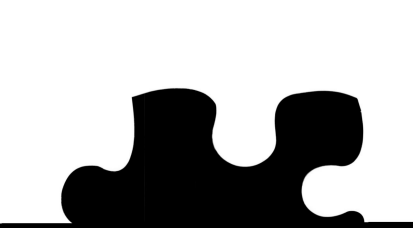

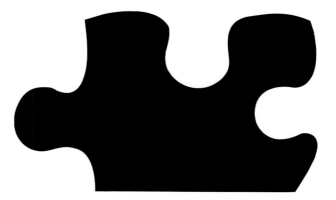

"**You live but once;
you might as well
be amusing.** "

COCO CHANEL

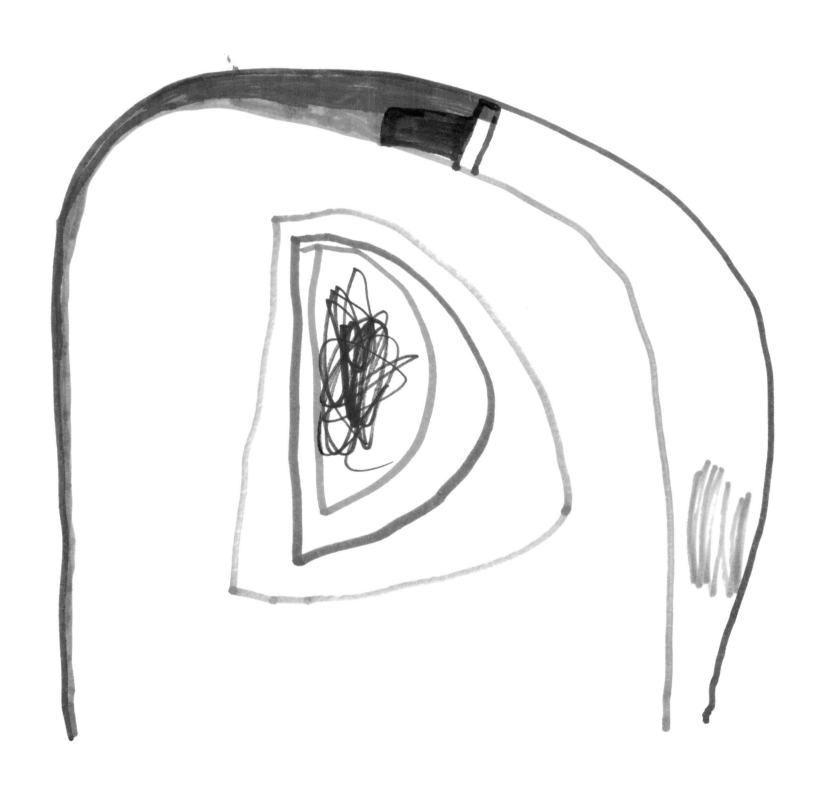

259

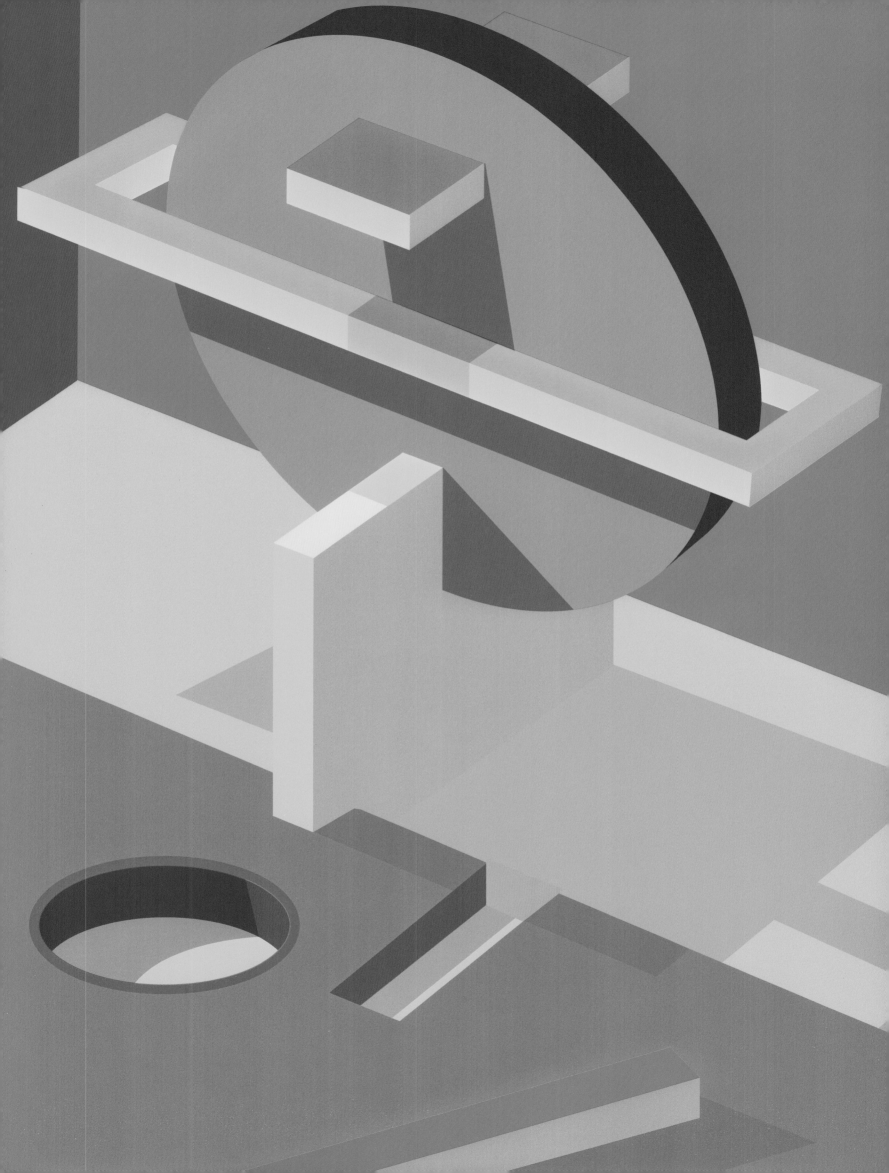

270
RIVERSIDE

LIKE NO OTH

THE BUILDIN

FOUR SEASO

RESIDENCES

NEW ORLEAN

FOUR SEASONS
HOTEL AND PRIVATE RESIDENCES
NEW ORLEANS

PITNEY BOWES • PITNEY BOWES • PITNEY BOWES • PITNEY BOWES • PITNEY BOWES • PITNEY BOWES

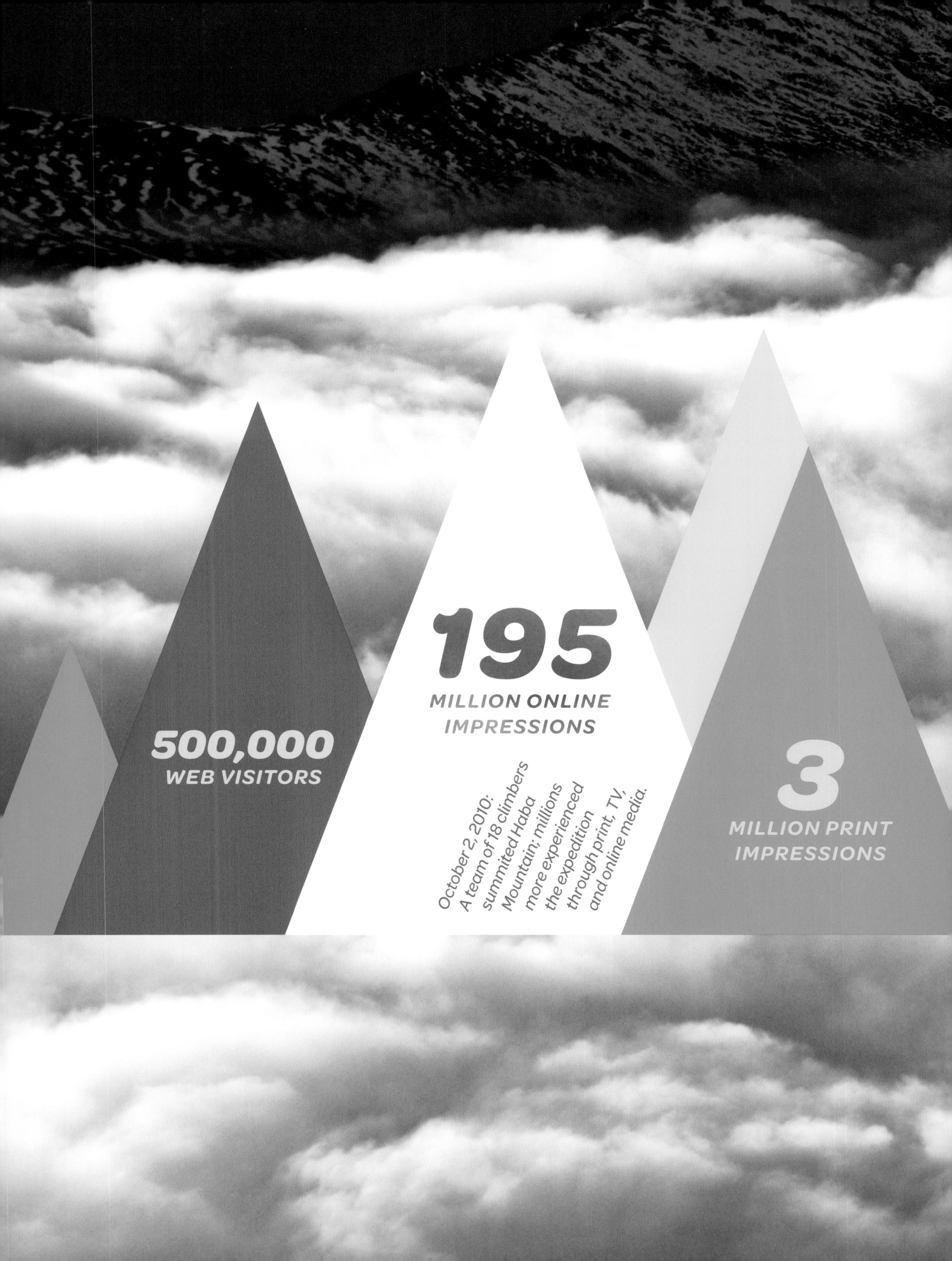

500,000
WEB VISITORS

195
MILLION ONLINE
IMPRESSIONS

October 2, 2010:
A team of 18 climbers
summited Haba
Mountain; millions
more experienced
the expedition
through print, TV,
and online media.

3
MILLION PRINT
IMPRESSIONS

> "Change almost never fails because it's too early. It almost always fails because it's too late."

SETH GODIN

222

W8

INDIGO	RED	PURPLE
PERIWINKLE	PINK	LAVENDER
SIENNA	APPLE RED	GRAPE
DUSTY ROSE	CORAL RED	VIOLET
COBALT	CRANBERRY	DARK PURPLE
ROYAL BLUE	PRIMROSE	REGAL PURPLE

Indigo Shades
Triadics

Red Shades
Split Complements

Purple Shades
Split Complements

LIME GREEN	WHITE	RED-ORANGE
SPRING GREEN	ALMOND	SALMON
CAMEL	BEIGE	WARM RED
MARIGOLD	COOL GRAY	SUNSET
PALM GREEN	TAUPE	RUBY
CHARTREUSE	LIGHT	STRAWBERRY

Lime Green Shades
Base Color

White Shades
Color Blends

Red-Orange Shades
Triadics

Shades of Lime Green and Purple connote artistic and innovative qualities.

Shades of Teal
express trustfulness..

BLACK SHADES
REGAL PURPLE + AQUA

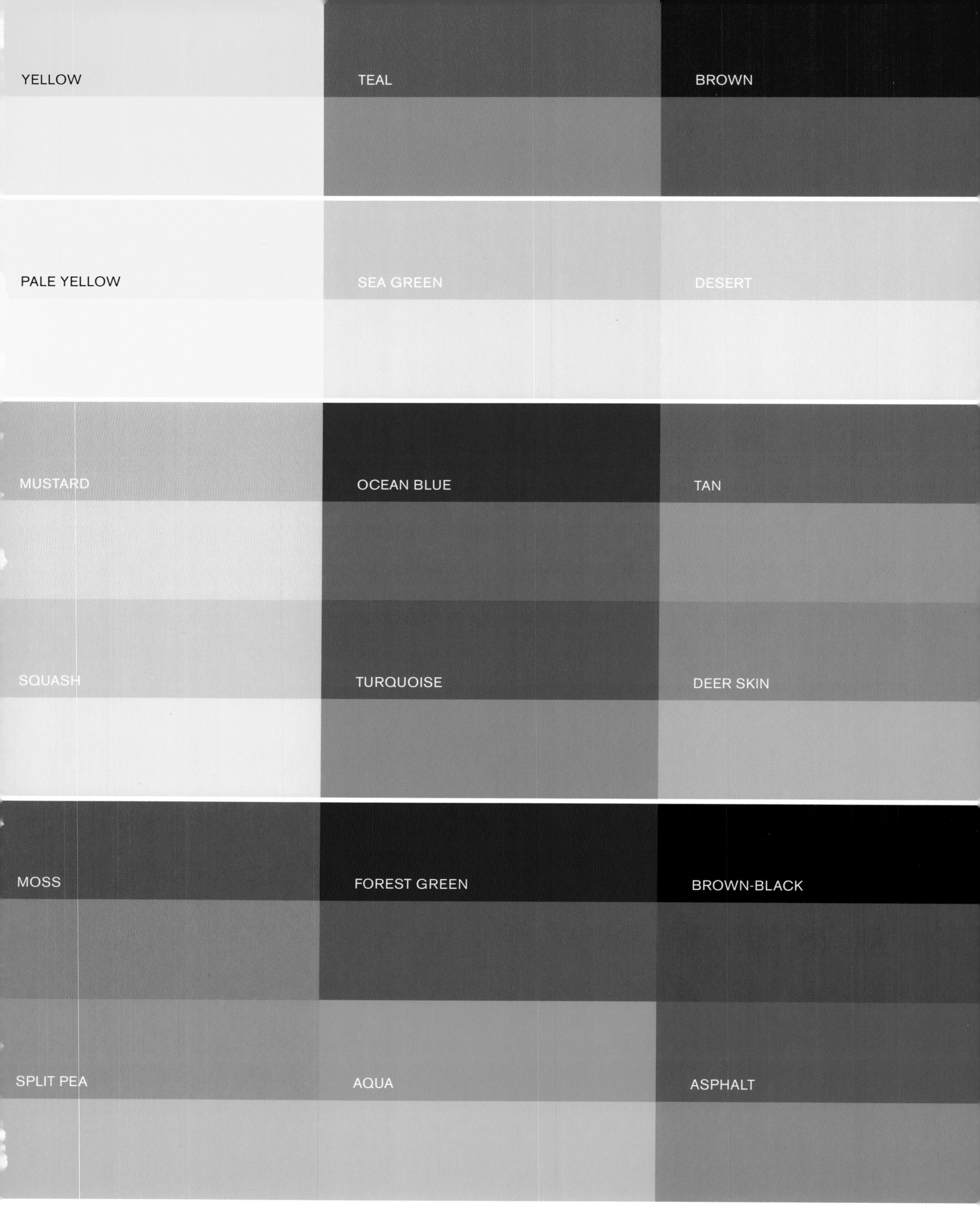

YELLOW	TEAL	BROWN
PALE YELLOW	SEA GREEN	DESERT
MUSTARD	OCEAN BLUE	TAN
SQUASH	TURQUOISE	DEER SKIN
MOSS	FOREST GREEN	BROWN-BLACK
SPLIT PEA	AQUA	ASPHALT

Yellow Shades
Triadics

Teal Shades
Split Complements

Brown Shades
Complements

BLACK	MAGENTA	GOLD
PEWTER	ORCHID	GOLDEN
GRAY	GARNET	BRONZE
WARM GRAY	ROSE	SAWGRASS
CHARCOAL	MULBERRY	LEAF
SILVER	AZALEA	BRIGHT GOLD

Black Shades
Complements

Magenta Shades
Complements

Gold Shades
Split Complements

Matthew Beals

■ Steelcase Design Partnership

901 44th Street SE PO Box 1967 Grand Rapids, MI 49501

Steelcase Design Partnership

Judi Kyler

■ Steelcase Design Partnership

Judi Kyler
858 South Front Street
Philadelphia, PA 19147
+1.215.465.0920 F +1.215.465.0929
judi.kyler@steelcase.com www.steelcase.com

Metro | Vecta | Brayton

858 South Front Street Philadelphia, PA 19147 +1.215.465.0920
F +1.215.465.0929 E judi.kyler@steelcase.com www.steelcase.com

Metro | Vecta | Brayton
516 West Encanto Boulevard Phoenix, AZ 85003 +1.602.254.1575
F +1.602.261.7963 C +1.602.684.8111 E matt.beals@steelcase.com www.steelcase.com

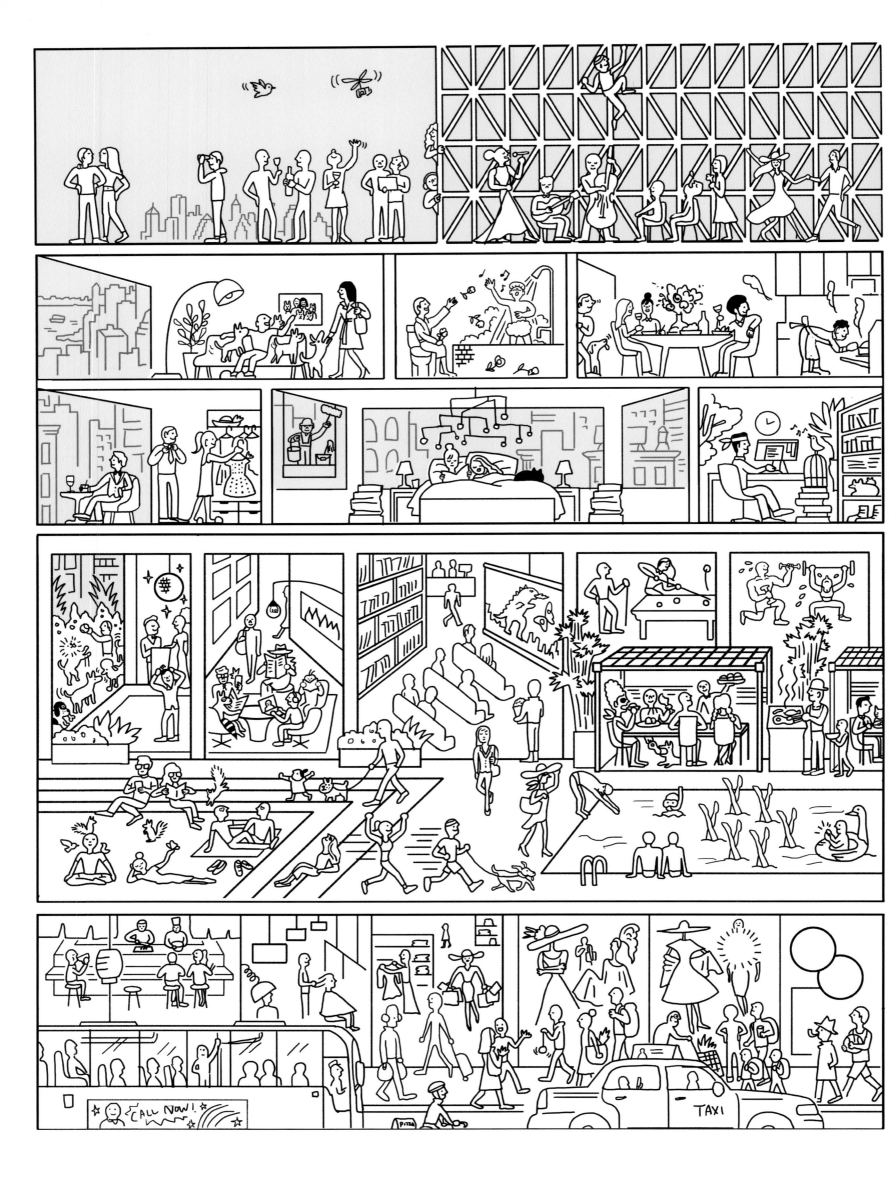

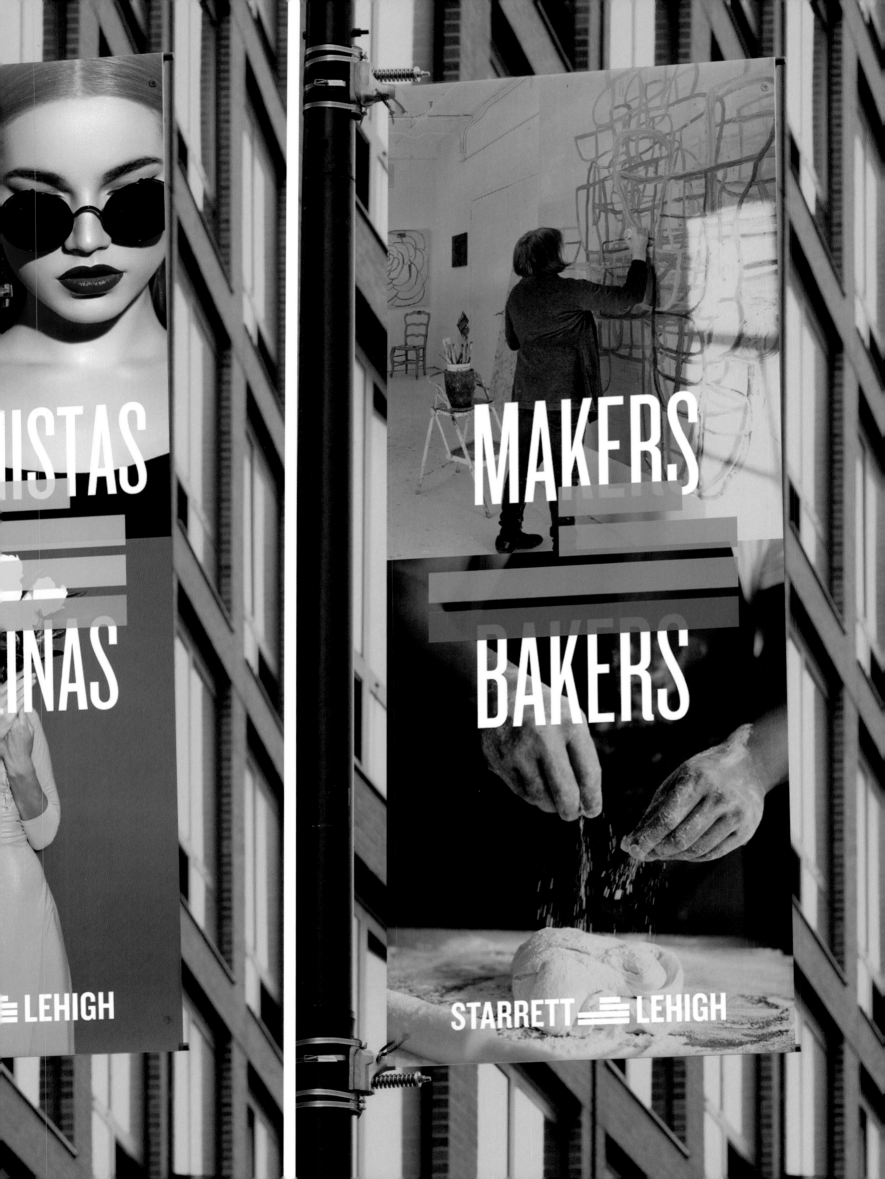

"Life isn't about waiting for the storm to pass... It's about learning to dance in the rain."

VIVIAN GREENE

CAPTIONS

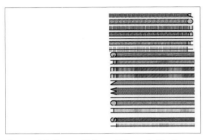

Greenwich Street, Tribeca / Vornado Realty Trust: original typographic illustration by Takahiro Kurashima

The Grace Building / Brookfield Properties: downward view of the building; original architectural photography by Alan Schindler

Left: The Holland / A&E Real Estate Holdings: logomark design
Right: Four Seasons Hotel and Private Residences New Orleans: original graphic illustration inspired by the building's architecture

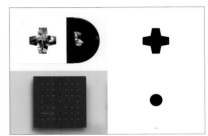

Four Seasons Hotel and Private Residences New Orleans: original graphic illustration inspired by the building's architecture; "Like No Other" box set, with custom die-cut pattern reflecting the building's unique cruciform shape

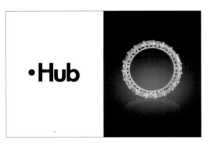

Left: Hub / Steiner Studios: logotype design emphasizing the site's central, transit-friendly location
Right: Diamond Eternity Band / Leo Ingwer Inc.: original photography by Antfarm

Left: Leo Ingwer Inc.: "Love Might Be Blind, But She's Not" consumer advertising
Right: The Austin San Francisco / Pacific Eagle Holdings Corporation: cover design referencing the site's location at the intersection of Pine and Polk

The Austin San Francisco / Pacific Eagle Holdings Corporation: "The characters of Lower Polk" original illustrations by CDR

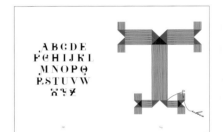

Left: 498 West End Avenue / Samson Management LLC: custom typographic design
Right: 19 Park Place / ABN Realty LLC: original typographic illustration

498 West End Avenue / Samson Management LLC:
Left: Emboss/deboss on cotton paper
Right: Custom laser-cut sleeve

Left: Leo Ingwer Inc.: diamond design in Art Deco style; original photography by Antfarm; custom composite by And Partners
Right: The North Face / VF Corporation: annual report design; original illustration by Chris Dent

222 West 80th Street / Friedland Properties: original photo rendering composite by Anders Overgaard and MARCH

222 West 80th Street / Friedland Properties: image that shows the making of original photo rendering composite by Anders Overgaard and MARCH

Janu Montenegro, the sister brand of Aman: signature image on cover of launch brochure with silver foil stamp/deboss; original photography by David Bellemere

Janu Montenegro, the sister brand of Aman: "Rethink Balance" original photography by David Bellemere, shot on location in Montenegro

Left: NYU Hospital for Joint Diseases, Center for Children: logomark design
Right: Original illustration by Eliana Schimmel

And Partners: "All things And" self-promotion

498 West End Avenue / Samson Management LLC: original illustrated map by Emily Robertson

Left: Jackson Park / Tishman Speyer: custom typography and logotype design
Right: 222 West 80th Street / Friedland Properties: original materials photography by Tom Hayes

The Chatsworth / HFZ Capital Group: photo rendering composite; original photography by Evan Joseph; composite by Imaginary Lines; rendering by MARCH

Left: 242 Broome Street / Taconic Investment Partners: cloth cover featuring logotype and copper foil/deboss with edge painting
Right: 1 Great Jones Alley / Madison Realty Capital: original materials photography in conjunction with BKSK Architects

270 Riverside Drive / 270 Holding LLC: original interior photography by Luca Pioltelli

8899 Beverly Boulevard / Townscape Partners: streetscape rendering by Binyan Studios

Left: Broadform: poster design featuring offset lithography with spot thermography
Right: SpecLogix: education series produced in conjunction with AIGA; stylized "G" referencing the blankets of a printing press

Missoni Baia / Edgewater Development: custom-designed children's splash-pad area; rendering by Moso Studio

Hub / Steiner Studios: custom typographic illustration

EŌS / The Durst Organization: "Billiards on Madison Park" original conceptual photography by Geof Kern; postproduction by Imaginary Lines

Garvies Point Master Plan / RXR Realty: original illustrated map by Josie Portillo

Left: One Bennett Park / Related Midwest: original illustration by Cassandre Montoriol
Right: 475 Clermont / RXR Realty: original wall mural by Mona Caron

261 Hudson / Related Companies: logotype design; original illustration by Bruno Grizzo

Left: Hub / Steiner Studios: original illustration by Tomi Um
Right: The Park Loggia at 15 West 61st Street / AvalonBay Communities: "Dancing on Broadway" original photo rendering composite by Liz Von Hoene and Binyan Studios

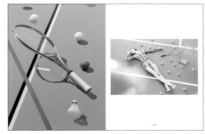

Missoni Baia / Edgewater Development:
Left: Original still-life photography by Richie Talboy
Right: Original fashion photography by Caroline Knopf; styling by Vanessa Reid

The Park Loggia at 15 West 61st Street / AvalonBay Communities: original illustration by Thomas Vielle

8899 Beverly Boulevard / Townscape Partners: rendering by Binyan Studios

Left: 212 West 93rd Street: "House of Cards" property brochure
Right: Jackson Park / Tishman Speyer: mobile website design; renderings by Volley Studio

Left: Transactional, multiplatform website for real estate industry
Right: Hub / Steiner Studios: unconventional, Mad Libs–style contact form

Left: West Hollywood, original photography by Andrew Macpherson
Right: Bryant Park, original photography by Alan Schindler

The Park Loggia at 15 West 61st Street / AvalonBay Communities. "Central Park Is So Close, It's in Your Living Room" original photo rendering composite; original photography by Liz Von Hoene and Binyan Studios

Jackson Park / Tishman Speyer: custom typography design

EŌS / The Durst Organization: "Golfing in Nomad" original conceptual photography by Geof Kern; postproduction by Imaginary Lines

Left: 222 West 80th Street / Friedland Properties: original materials photography by Tom Hayes
Right: Solé Mia / LeFrak and Turnberry: original illustration by Gabriella Marcella

Missoni Baia / Edgewater Development: fashion photography by Caroline Knopf; styling by Vanessa Reid

Left: 222 West 80th Street / Friedland Properties: original materials photography by Tom Hayes
Right: Missoni Baia / Edgewater Development: blind deboss and foil business cards with variable ombré patterning

Cavalleri Malibu / Pacific Eagle Holdings Corporation: website design; original photography by Emily Winiker; renderings by MARCH

EŌS / The Durst Organization: "Life Inside and Out" brochure with sewn spine, featuring an unconventional approach to a fact sheet; original conceptual photography by Geof Kern; postproduction by Imaginary Lines

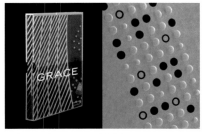

Left: The Grace / Brookfield Properties: custom Lucite slipcase with etched original photography by Alan Schindler
Right: Broadform: blind emboss and foil stamping on FiberMark

EŌS / The Durst Organization: "Celebration Underwater" original conceptual photography by Geof Kern; postproduction by Imaginary Lines

1 Great Jones Alley / Madison Realty Capital: wet-spa rendering by MARCH

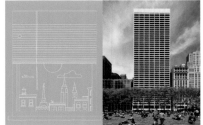

Left: Fordham Law School's: "The Network Effect" original illustration by Ben Wiseman
Right: The Grace Building / Brookfield Properties: original architectural photography by Alan Schindler

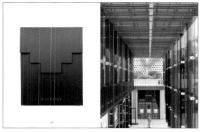

Left: Riverbank / MassMutual: custom die-cut folder, referencing the Riverbank building's crown
Right: Miami Design District, original photography by Jason Schmidt

Original illustrations produced in-house
Left: "Thinking Creatively" at Kean University
Right: Guy Carpenter

Left: 78 Irving / Madison Realty Capital: custom typography design
Right: Ransom Everglades School: registered deboss and lithography cover

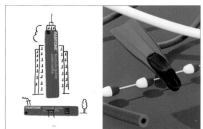

Left: Pantone: "Advantages of Size" global advertising campaign to relaunch the Pantone Matching System fan guides; "Livin' Large" illustrations by Seymour Chwast
Right: Missoni Baia / Edgewater Development: still-life photography by Richie Talboy

Solé Mia / LeFrak and Turnberry: original illustrated site plan map by Nancy Howell

Manhattan View / SCG America: "The Height of Living" original photo illustration composite by Jason Schmidt and Sara Shakeel

Left: Missoni Baia / Edgewater Development: original illustration (with sketch overlay) by Olimpia Zagnoli
Right: Watermark Seaport / Skanska: wordmark design

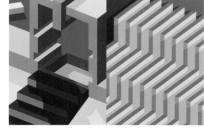

The JACX / Tishman Speyer: "Where Innovators Play" original illustrations by Richard Keeling

Left: 85 lamps by Droog from And Partners'
original studio
Right: 1 Great Jones Alley / Madison Realty
Capital: cover design with custom logotype in
pearl foil; hero rendering by MARCH

Left: The Easton / Related Companies:
original photography by Clarke Tolton
Right: Pierrepont / Jonathan Rose Companies:
original illustration produced in-house

8899 Beverly Boulevard / Townscape Partners:
Left: Original still-life photography by
Andrew Macpherson
Right: Entry rendering by Binyan Studios

8899 Beverly Boulevard / Townscape Partners:
rendering by Binyan Studios

Left: 8899 Beverly Boulevard / Townscape
Partners: original still-life photography by
Brooke Holm
Right: Professional Bank: "Bank with Interesting"
strategic brand design

Left: Janu Montenegro, the sister brand of
Aman: general advertising
Right: Neenah Paper: "1/2 the Job" paper
promotion with custom lettering / foil and
die-cut cover

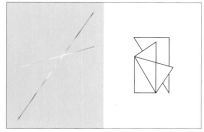

Fifteen Fifty Van Mission / Related California:
original graphic illustration and logomark design

8899 Beverly Boulevard / Townscape Partners:
motor-court rendering by Binyan Studios

One Bennett Park / Related Companies:
naming and brand creation, featuring
various specialty techniques

Left: Hub / Steiner Studios: rendering by
Volley Studio
Right: Missoni Baia / Edgewater Development:
original materials photography by Richie Talboy

Left: 1 Great Jones Alley / Madison Realty
Capital: master bath rendering by MARCH
Right: 845 West End Avenue / Atlas Capital /
Sterling Properties: custom typography and
foil-stamped cover design

Janu Montenegro, the sister brand of Aman:
architectural rendering by Hayes Davidson

Los Angeles skyline, original photography by
Andrew Macpherson

NCJW Journal: "Find Your Voice"
benchmark campaign; photographs from
Getty Images

Left: 261 Hudson / Related Companies:
original illustration by Bruno Grizzo
Right: Aman Resorts: custom application design

VF Corporation: annual report design;
custom typography and art direction; image is
courtesy of Vans

"From West to East":
Left: 610 West 110th Street / Urban
American: letterpressed logotype
Right: The Easton / Related Companies:
logotype design

Left: And Partners: identity design, 2002
Right: And Partners: identity design, 2009

Left: "The Blind Side" by Michael Lewis / W. W.
Norton: original hand lettering for book cover
Right: Pantone: "Advantages of Size" global
advertising campaign to relaunch Pantone
Matching System fan guides; "Big Advantage"
original illustrations by Seymour Chwast

15 Hubert Street / Samson Management LLC:
Left: Original photography by Jason Schmidt
Right: Custom typography and logotype design

Left: Neenah Paper: Classic Crest promotion
Right: Missoni Baia / Edgewater Development: cards with original illustration by Olimpia Zagnoli; lithography with spot foil stamping

Sage Hill School: original illustrated map by Nana Rausch

Left: The Mart: naming and logotype design
Right: 1 Columbus Place / The Brodsky Organization: logotype design with blind emboss and foil stamp deboss

The Sunshine Gala / Books for Kids: original illustration/serigraph, 2005

Left: 261 Hudson / Related Companies: original photography by Jacob Pritchard
Right: Pantone: "Advantages of Size" global advertising campaign to relaunch the Pantone Matching System fan guides; "Color Full" original illustration by Seymour Chwast

Left: Delta Asset Management: logotype and identity system; photography by Photonica
Right: JBG Smith: dynamic identity system design

And Partners: self-promotion poster for opening party, printed with fluorescent ink

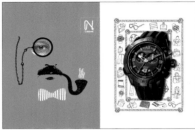

Left: Neenah Cabinet: original illustration by Oliver Munday
Right: Nautica / VF Corporation: annual report; original illustration by Chris Dent

EŌS / The Durst Organization: "Dinner Party" original conceptual photography by Geof Kern; postproduction by Imaginary Lines

Left: NCJW Journal: "Building Bridges, Bridging Divides" cover design; original illustration by Luba Lukova
Right: The Sunshine Gala / Books for Kids: serigraph for 20th anniversary

Left: And Partners' studio, 1999, with Vitra Wiggle Side Chair by Frank Gehry
Right: 222 West 80th Street / Friedland Properties: original materials photography by Tom Hayes

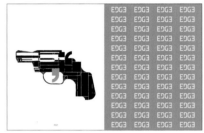

Left: Punc't / Neenah Paper: apostrophe poster by Stefan Sagmeister; part of the "Putting Punctuation in Its Place" series
Right: EDGE / Douglaston Development: palindrome logotype design

Left: Ask Mohawk Series / Mohawk Fine Papers: copywriting and design
Right: The JACX / Tishman Speyer: "Jacks" fabricated by Kaiser Suidan

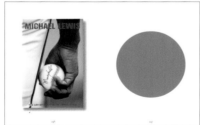

Left: "Moneyball" by Michael Lewis / W. W. Norton: original hand lettering for book cover; image from Getty Images
Right: Punc't / Neenah Paper: "Red Period" design; part of the "Putting Punctuation in Its Place" series

"Peace" / AOL: holiday promotion featuring individual illustrations for each of the media company's properties; original illustration by Seymour Chwast

"Peace" / AOL: holiday promotion featuring individual illustrations for each of the media company's properties; original illustration by Seymour Chwast

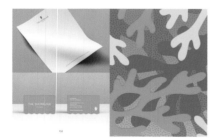

The Shoreline at Solé Mia / LeFrak and Turnberry:
Left: Naming and brand development, including scalloped die-cut business card
Right: Original illustration by Gabriella Marcella

Left: Jackson Park / Tishman Speyer: art activation by R Robots
Right: The Surf Lodge: art activation (detail) by Jen Stark
Both: Eric Firestone, art consultant

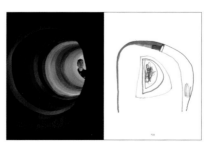

Left: The Surf Lodge: art activation by Jen Stark
Right: Original illustration by Sophia Schimmel

The JACX / Tishman Speyer: "Where Innovators Play" original illustrations by Richard Keeling

Missoni Baia / Edgewater Development:
Left: Original illustration by Olimpia Zagnoli
Right: Original still-life photography by
Richie Talboy

Left: 270 Riverside Drive / 270 Holdings LLC:
original photography by Luca Pioltelli
Right: Four Seasons Hotel and Private Residences
New Orleans: tablet website design

Left: Pitney Bowes: foil stamping with emboss/
deboss combination
Right: VF Corporation: original information
graphics

Left: The Park Loggia at 15 West 61st Street
/ AvalonBay Communities: rendering by
Binyan Studios
Right: 222 West 80th Street / Friedland Properties:
logotype design, referencing the site's large
windows through an aperture icon

The Park Loggia at 15 West 61st Street /
AvalonBay Communities: "A Grand Arrival"
original photo rendering composite by
Liz Von Hoene and Binyan Studios

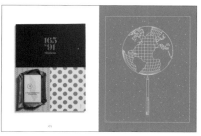

Left: Mirabeau / A&E Real Estate Holdings:
cover with die-cut scores that breaks into 3
smaller books (brochure, pad and neighborhood
pocket guide)
Right: Fordham Law School: original illustration
by Ben Wiseman

Neenah Paper: "Olive Is Not Drab"
color-psychology promotion, produced
in conjunction with Dewey Sadka

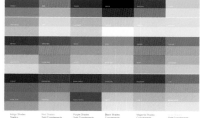

Neenah Paper: "Olive Is Not Drab"
color-psychology promotion, produced
in conjunction with Dewey Sadka

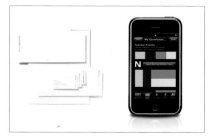

Left: Steelcase: branding and corporate
identity, featuring engraved stationery
Right: Neenah Paper: "Color Unleashed"
color-palette building iPhone application,
one of the first of its kind in the App Store

Pier 57's Super Pier / RXR Realty:
art activation by Carlos Zamora

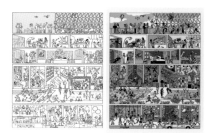

Hub / Steiner Studios: original illustrations
by Tomi Um

Solé Mia / LeFrak and Turnberry: original
hand-lettered logotype by Nancy Howell;
original lifestyle photography by Harrison Boyce

Starrett-Lehigh / RXR Realty: brand
development featuring various photographs
with surprising, witty message pairings

CREDITS

And Partners Team Members
Past and Present

Shigeto Akiyama
Christiane Allen
Matthew Anderson
Tiffany Bachman
Craig Bailey
Nate Baltikas
Gabriella Bar-Lavi
Josh Berta
Nada Bibi
Nina Boesch
Michael Braley
Colleen Branigan
Donovan Brien
Susan Brzozowski
Gwen Bueno de Mesquita
Jamie Carey
Chuck Carrasco-Rudy
Vanessa Chiulli
Teeraporn Chomdej
Christine Chow
Sarah Coffman
Warren Corbitt
Valerie Courtney
Brian Crooks
Caitlin Daly
Katia Davidson Ferrara
Nicholas Davidson
Melissa DeAsis
Beverly Desoto
Korly DeVries
Evan Dody
Sara Dunberg
Matt Fiocca
Olivia Flory
Megan Forb
Flannery Foster Ringgenberg
Lauren Gabbe-Greene

Thom Geraghty
Charisse Gibilisco
Alison Greenberg
Shana Gurkova
Sarah Hans
Candice Heberer
Caroline Hodge
Sarah Hollowood
Su Hong
Michael Houston
Judy Hsu
Albert Ignacio
Karen Ires
Norman Ibarra
Martin Iselt
Jeff Jarvis
Amy Johnson
Lynelle Nicole Johnson
Miriam Kaplan
Rachel Kashon
Mor Keshet
Alison Ketchledge
Linnea Keys
Leeana Khalique
Ishan Khosla
Susanna Ko
Lisa Koenigsberg-Turek
Chris Korbey
Lindsay Kunkle
Jessica Lasorsa
Josh Levi
Giona Lodigiani
Kassandra Lombard
Antonio Mah
Chris Manlapid
Nina Mata
Maureen McLaughlin

Tiffany Meyers
Chris Miller
Kathy Molinaro
Katie Morabito
Kristen Nagy
Jonathan Newman
Thomas Ng
Mikayla Nissan
Thanyanun Nopmaneerasmee
Amy Novak
Andrew Park
Lisa Paruch
Madeline Press
Steve Renn
Marissa Samsky
Ana Claudia Schultz
Aimee Sealfon Kassana
Deborah Short
Amanda Siebert
Felicia Soto
Brett Tabolt
Eiji Tsuda
Angela Tyler
Josef Valu
Charlie Veprek
Andrew Vickers
Laura Lee Vo
Emily Wais
Ginny Wang
Jarrett White
Sarah White
Mollie Wilkie
Brooke Willis
Roger Wong
Monika Zareba

Strategic Partners

A to A Studio Solutions, Ltd.
Vit Abramovich
Beth Adams
Munawar Ahmed
Aldine Printing
Aaron Alexander
Ambassador Arts
Joey Arak
Arquitectonica
Art Dept / Illustration Dept
Art Guild
ArX Solutions
Asymptote Architecture
AV&C
Holga Balina
Raul Barreneche
Mimi Bean
John Becker
David Bellemere
Francesca Bergamini
Hali Berman
Bernstein & Andriulli
David Bianciardi
Michael Bierut
Bill Rooney Studio
Binyan Studios
BKSK Architects
Carole Bloom
Harrison Boyce
Brilliant Graphics
Jeff Broder
Broder Productions
Steven Brower
Debby Brown
Cammisa Buerhaus
David Bullock
David Butterworth
CambridgeSeven
Lath Carlson
Mona Caron
Cervera Real Estate
CetraRuddy Architecture
Claudia Chaback

Marcos Chin
Seymour Chwast
Kevin Cimini
Citi Habitats
CJ Graphics
Clodagh Design
Coe Displays
Joseph Cohen
Compass
CookFox Architects
The Corcoran Group
Corcoran Sunshine Marketing Group
DataGraphic
Roberto de Vicq de Cumptich
Chris Dent
Gary Dickson
Dickson's Inc.
Douglas Elliman Development Marketing
Greg Duncan
Aaron Dussair
Paul Earle Jr.
Karen Eckelmeyer
Edmonds + Lee Architects
Elastic Architects
Electrosonic
Jonathan Elmore
Enea Garden Design
John Evangelista
David Fells
Aaron Feng
Fey Printing
Eric Firestone
Jean Fontana
Richard Frank
Friend & Johnson
Bill Gallery
Scott Gasch
Guillaume Gaudet
Steff Geissbühler
Alexander Gelman
Gensler
Carin Goldberg
Grade Architects

Bruno Grizzo
Shijia Gu
Scott Guerin
Jennifer Hajar
Spiros Halaris
Mike Hall
Halstead Property Development Marketing
Handel Architects
Tim Hayes
Hayes Davidson
Hemlock Printers
Katie Hepp
Brandon Hicks
Delphine Hirasuna
HMWhite
Brooke Holm
Nancy Howell
Jackie Hsia
Ken Hunter
Michael Ian Kaye
Igicom
Mirko Ilić
Imaginary Lines
Alexander Isley
Ismael Leyva Architects
Denis Jakuc
Gordana Jelisijevic
Justin Jewett
Evan Joseph
Christina Kapinos
Brooks Kaya
Richard Keeling
Geof Kern
Chip Kidd
Kinlin Rutherfurd Architects
Holly Kirby
Kirkwood
Justin Kitrosser
Mike Klausmeier
Knightsbridge Park
David Kohler
Stephanie Koleda
Daniel Korte

Strategic Partners (continued)

Frits Kouwenhoven

Dick Kouwenhoven

Alyson Kuhn

Takahiro Kurashima

Abbey Kuster-Prokell

David Lee Meyers

Sari Levy-Schorr

Ashleigh Lindenauer

Lithographix

Luba Lukova

M18

Peter Madlinger

Ray Mancini

Enrique Mangalindan

Gabriella Marcella

March

Daniel Margolin

The Mark Company

Marmol Radziner

Marvel Architects

Carlo McCormick

Andrew Macpherson

Milton X. Melendez

Michael Van Valkenburgh Associates

Heidi Mitchell

Bryn Mooth

Moso Studio

MPress

Oliver Munday

Nancy Packes Signature Marketing Services

Emily Oberman

ODA Architecture

Olson Kundig

Frank Oswald

Anders Overgaard

James Owen

Chris Ozer

Spyridon Pagkalis

Pamela Burton & Company

Paris Forino

Anna Parry

Pembrooke & Ives

Luca Pioltelli

Woody Pirtle

PKSB Architects

Matthew Porter

Sam Potts

Byron Racki

RAMSA

Lauren Rasken

Nana Rausch

Revuelta

Revuelta Architecture International

Konstantina Revythi

Julia Rexon

Vincent Ricardel

Emily Robertson

Rocket Society Industries

Allison Romang

Miranda Römer

Seth Rosner

Massimo Russo

Naomi Ryan

Dewey Sadka

Sage AV

Stefan Sagmeister

Maria Santana

Tim Saputo

Bob Schaeffer

Paula Scher

Denise Schiffer

Jason Schmidt

Justin Schwartz

Jared Seeger

Josh Senior

Senior Post

Joe Sgroe

Samer Shaath

Sara Shakeel

Alexia Valentina Sheinman

SHoP Architects

SLCE Architects

Tyler Small

Dave Smith

Martin Solarte

Oscar Solarte

SOM

Sotheby's International Realty

Iva Spitzer

Todd St. John

Daniela Stallinger

Stephen Starbuck

Jen Stark

Chris Stoll

Hicks Stone

Dave Storey

Scott Stowell

Kaiser Suidan

Jenny Sullivan

Richie Talboy

Michael Tavani

Walter Thomas

Noel Tocci

Clarke Tolton

Bob Tursack

Tomi Um

Robert Valentine

Mary van de Wiel

Carin Van Vuuren

James Victore

Thomas Vielle

Terry Villani

The Villani Group

Volley Studio

Liz Von Hoene

Adam Wahler

Alan Wahler

Rachael Wang

Charles Ward

Rebecca Weinberg

Emily Winiker

Chris Wormell

Thomas Wright

Yabu Pushelberg

Olimpia Zagnoli

Carlos Zamora

ABOUT AND PARTNERS

And Partners is a New York City-based strategic design firm. They work with leaders in a variety of industries to build businesses, create and differentiate brands, and command a premium in the marketplace. Since 1999, the firm has developed a methodology that integrates strategy, design, innovation and technology to help their clients intelligently evolve, grow and succeed in an ever-changing world.

DAVID SCHIMMEL
Founder and President / Creative Director

David combines creative thinking with pragmatic business acumen to help clients understand and capitalize on trends in the marketplace. Under his leadership, And Partners has become an internationally recognized branding consultancy that blends traditional design discipline with innovative technology and interactive design. David works with brands across various industries in the premium consumer and professional service space. His work has been recognized with prestigious communications awards such as a One Show Gold Pencil at the One Club and a Yellow Pencil from the British Design and Art Direction Awards, as well as numerous awards from PRINT, HOW, Communication Arts, Type Directors Club and Graphis. He is a graduate of Washington University in St. Louis, with degrees in Communication Design and Business, and founded And Partners at age 23.

Covers: Camouflage pattern by
David Schimmel & Thanyanun Nopmaneerasmee

© 2019 Assouline Publishing
3 Park Avenue, 27th floor
New York, NY 10016 USA
Tel.: 212-989-6769 Fax: 212-647-0005
www.assouline.com

Art Direction by David Schimmel
Design by Thanyanun Nopmaneerasmee

Printed in the United States by Kirkwood
ISBN: 9781614289005

All rights reserved.
No part of this publication may be reproduced or
transmitted in any form or by any means, electronic
or otherwise, without prior consent of the publisher.